Sue Kreitzman is the author of five cookery books published in the United States: *The Nutrition Cookbook*, *Sunday Best*, *Garlic*, *Deli* and *Comfort Food*. Her past experience includes working for the *Atlanta Weekly* as food editor, co-founding and co-editing a restaurant review newsletter, directing a cookery school, being chef for a year at an elegant Atlanta restaurant, and teaching Food in Literature seminars at Emory University. She has written countless articles for newspapers and magazines across the United States.

Sue Kreitzman lives in East Anglia with her husband, nutrition scientist Dr Stephen Kreitzman, and her son Shawm, a dedicated horn student.

SUE KREITZMAN'S

Cambridge

Slim Cuisine

DELICIOUSLY SATISFYING RECIPES THAT KEEP YOU SLIM FOREVER

CORGI BOOKS

To ANH
with love and thanks

SUE KREITZMAN'S CAMBRIDGE SLIM CUISINE
A CORGI BOOK 0 552 13184 9

First publication in Great Britain

PRINTING HISTORY

Corgi edition published 1988

This book is set in 11/12 Linotron Palatino

Corgi Books are published by Transworld Publishers Ltd.,
61–63 Uxbridge Road, Ealing, London W5 5SA, in Australia by
Transworld Publishers (Australia) Pty. Ltd., 15–23 Helles
Avenue, Moorebank NSW 2170, and in New Zealand by Transworld
Publishers (N.Z.) Ltd., Cnr. Moselle and Waipareira Avenues,
Henderson, Auckland.

Printed in Great Britain by
Redwood Burn Limited, Trowbridge, Wiltshire and
bound by Pegasus Bookbinding, Melksham, Wiltshire.

Contents

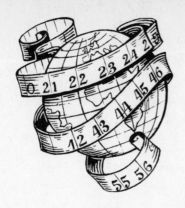

Acknowledgements

I could never have survived the endless testing, experimenting and tasting involved in this project without the loyal, cheerful and completely supportive help of my staff. A thousand thankyous to Penny Roseveare, my secretary/assistant, who coddled the Slim Cuisine manuscript as if it were her own, kept me organized, took recipes home to test on her family, and exhibited an enthusiasm for the project that warmed the cockles of my heart. A thousand more to Mary Hardy, my housekeeper, who patiently prevented my intensely busy kitchen from descending into chaos, generously ladled out plenty of enthusiasm of her own, and has been an invaluable part, of the Slim Cuisine tasting panel, and still another thousand to Sandy Perry who has demonstrated a wonderful talent and affinity for Slim Cuisine, and has been an excellent addition to the kitchen team.

Heartfelt thanks as well to Tessa Prior, Ginny Broad and Roger Howard at Cambridge Nutrition for their support for the project; to Peter and Mary Dean for their warmth, friendship and good sense; to Shashi Rattan for Indian cookery advice and for generously sharing her family's special recipes; to Eleanor Harnish, for finding Tiptoft and for friendship; to Ian Hendry, for producing a dazzling Slim Cuisine buffet; to John Jones for his generous and expert help; to Shawn and his family at Swann's The Butcher in Newmarket, for patiently answering endless questions about British cuts of meat; to the Stokes for 100 lb of King Edward potatoes, one of the most satisfying gifts I've ever received; and to the Niemans for the bagels.

A special thankyou to Cambridge Diet Counsellors: the Webbers, the Mauders, the Tuckers, the Hartleys, the Haindls, the

Barrys, the Harts, the Weissingers and all the rest of you who came to my lectures and demonstrations, and made me feel abundantly welcome in England, my new home. This book is for you. Alan N. Howard and the people at Cambridge Nutrition believe strongly in sensible lifetime weight maintenance. I am very grateful to them for their commitment to and support for Slim Cuisine. Without them, this project would not have been possible.

Fervent thanks to Margaret Pedersen for spending two weeks at Tiptoft, shackled to the computer, meticulously using the Nutran Program to analyse each Slim Cuisine recipe for fat and Calorie counts. It was intense and exhausting and I am forever grateful.

And finally, thankyou to my husband, Steve, and my son, Shawm, who enrich my life; to Shallot, who loved my cooking to the very end; and to Sammy, who knows that Winalot mixed with roasted garlic is doggie ambrosia.

Preface

'Cookery writers are these days expected,
I fear, to save the contemporary soul, which now
inhabits the waistline.'

Jane Grigson – *Observer* Sunday Magazine, 11th January 1987

'Never Trust a Skinny Cook.' The words were embroidered on my aprons and emblazoned on my soul. There I was, 210 pounds (15 stone) of rotund, bursting-at-the-seams womanhood, cooking up a storm of goodies all absolutely delicious and utterly fattening. When I saw the light and shed 5½ stone on the Cambridge Diet I threw out all my aprons with their obsolete embroideries, but I was left with a problem. Both the 15 stone and my profession of food writer were a result of my passion for food. The passion was still there along with a new one – the burning desire to remain slim. Can one indulge both such passions simultaneously? Is it possible to satisfy a hunger for deep, rich and complex flavours and still maintain a newly sylphlike figure? I am here to tell you that it can be done. All my professional (and passionate) skill has been devoted to developing a new maintenance cuisine. A cuisine that utilizes techniques enabling the cook to produce tantalizing and delicious dishes that are low in Calories (especially empty Calories and fat Calories), high in nutrition, yet eminently satisfying. These cookery methods can be used for all the family, even family members with no weight problems. My methods comprise a healthier way of preparing food that benefits everyone, even those who do not have to watch every Calorie, and the food is so good that no one will feel deprived.

I think of myself as a 210-pound woman in a size 10 body. Since I have begun cooking Slim Cuisine exclusively, those looming lost pounds have been kept at bay. What joy it is to be able to feast heartily, to enjoy large satisfying portions of my favourite foods, without suffering that all-too-familiar, inexorable, and demoralizing weight regain. For the first time in my life, I'm off the dieter's classic see-saw.

The basic premise of Slim Cuisine is that Dietary Fat is a villain. At more than twice the number of Calories per gram as carbohydrate and protein, it is a significant contributor to obesity. Even worse, it is considered to be one of the biggest cardiac risks. And, in addition to heart and blood vessel disease, it has been linked to several kinds of cancer. Not just the saturated animal fats. There are health problems with monounsaturated fats and polyunsaturated fats too. And it doesn't matter if you're cooking with butter, margarine, sunflower oil, yak fat or blubber – it still has a dense 9 Calories per gram – and these Calories go straight to your hips with deadly efficiency.

The NACNE Report in the UK and the American Heart Association in the USA recommend a dietary fat level of no more than 30 percent of total Calories. Slim Cuisine brings the fat levels down to below that point, yet it avoids the stultifying boredom that will engulf the desperate foodie who may gamely try to eat his or her way through other low-fat diets. Why will this regime succeed where others have caused terminal boredom and eventual failure? Because it pioneers the use of a whole battery of cookery techniques that enable the cook to eliminate added cooking fat altogether, yet retain the ravishing richness that foodies crave. The techniques save hundreds, sometimes thousands of Calories in a day's eating, yet they enable the cook to prepare compelling, rich-tasting, satisfying food, even though the added fat is missing. The techniques are simple and they form the basis of a whole lifetime of healthy eating.

It must be stressed that this maintenance programme, although an incredible boon to chronic dieters (no matter what their chosen weight-loss diet), is not for those dieters alone. Everyone will benefit significantly from eating this way. The recipes are Calorie and fat shy, yet nutrient dense. Sugar and salt have been drastically reduced too, yet there is enough taste, and texture to knock your socks off. Some recipes are for family-type meals, others are for elegant entertaining. There is plenty of 'junk-food': hamburgers, chips, pizza and icecream, and there is even a clutch of curries. And the best news is this: if you have been living on a high-fat diet, and switch to Slim Cuisine, you will *lose* weight painlessly and happily.

Each recipe in this book has Calorie and fat counts, and – when appropriate and interesting – comparison fat and Calorie levels for the traditional version of the recipe. Do remember, however, that compulsive Calorie counting is self-defeating and horribly tedious. If you eliminate high-fat ingredients and high-fat cookery methods, Calories take care of themselves. It *is* fun, though, to contrast the Calorie and fat levels in the traditional version of a recipe and the Slim Cuisine version. How delightful and comforting to know that one can feast on pesto, mashed potatoes, lasagne, even chips, without a qualm.

'Sam, we can't starve the boy,' Ethel protested. 'If he wants pie, let him have some. You're carrying this reducing fetish too far.'

Robert Silverberg – *The Iron Chancellor*, 1958

Essential Fatty Acids

A totally fat-free diet would be almost impossible to achieve. No one should even attempt such a diet; it would be dangerous. A certain amount of essential fatty acids are necessary each day to maintain health. There is no need to worry about fatty acid levels on the Slim Cuisine regime. The vegetables, grains, fish, meats and poultry you will be consuming contain more than enough of the essential fats. *Added* fats are not necessary. This is not just a guess or wishful conjecture. All Slim Cuisine recipes have been computer-analysed. Further checking was done by sending samples of many cooked recipes to an independent laboratory for analysis. The fatty acids necessary for good health were shown to be present in ample quantity.

Introduction by Dr A. N. Howard

I have known Sue Kreitzman since 1982 when I was working with her husband, Dr Steve Kreitzman, in connection with research on the Cambridge Diet in the United States. When visiting her house in Atlanta, I had the pleasure of eating several of her mouth-watering meals, which I can assure you were not based on Calorie counting. You could feel her enthusiasm for excellently prepared food, and its attractive presentation. I was not surprised to learn that she was the author of numerous best-selling cookery books and was well known in the USA as a food writer.

Since Sue joined our Research and Development Department at Cambridge Nutrition Ltd, in England, as Manager of Culinary Development, I have been impressed by her dedication, enthusiasm and complete determination to develop recipes and methods of achieving low-fat, low-Calorie dishes which at the same time were still absolutely delicious. In fact, having observed Sue at work for the past few years, she reminds me very much of any scientist tackling any difficult problem.

During the last ten years there has been a new revolution in our ideas about healthy eating. At one time it was thought that provided you included in your diet all the nutrients you needed, that was sufficient for good nutrition. Now we realize that over-consumption of some food ingredients is equally bad, the chief offender being fat – or, more precisely, saturated fat. In the Westernized world, 40 per cent of the Calories we consume is fat and, of this, the higher proportion is animal fat. The latter contains so-called 'saturated fatty acids', which in excess are harmful to health.

Too much fat in the diet can contribute to obesity, coronary heart disease, and some forms of cancer (particularly of the colon). Health authorities throughout the world are now suggesting that we should cut down the amount of fat we eat by as much as half. Of special interest to all of us is that over-consumption of fat is the main reason why people become overweight. Fried foods, especially chips, potato crisps, foods fried in butter, pies, fatty croissants, Danish pastries and sausage rolls are very high in Calories – the reason being that they are very fatty, and contribution of fat to Calories is twice that of other food ingredients. But there are many ordinary dishes which are equally fatty without people knowing it, because of the hidden fat used in cooking or which is present in ingredients.

When people lose weight on the Cambridge Diet, they look forward to the day when they can start eating normally again. But we know that if they eat exactly what they did before dieting, all the weight returns again. The only way people can maintain their weight is by consuming fewer Calories than they did before starting to diet. We estimate that for every 10 lb lost it is necessary to reduce one's intake by 100 Calories. An easy way to achieve this is by using the Cambridge Slim Cuisine – a new way of eating – developed by Sue Kreitzman. What she has done most remarkably is to cut down drastically and in some cases eliminate completely the quantity of fat in different dishes, without affecting their taste and appearance. Therefore you can eat a well-known dish and find it tastes delicious, is visually attractive, but often contains only half or less of the usual Calories.

To take many of the most popular dishes of the world and to leave out the fat in such a way that they taste good is a remarkable accomplishment requiring expert skill and ingenuity. Sue Kreitzman is to be congratulated on achieving a solution to one of the most important health problems of the age – the reduction of fat intake without depriving the consumer of the taste of real food.

I heartily recommend this book to all Cambridge Dieters. It is an excellent guide to the art of Cambridge Slim Cuisine. It represents a new culinary way of life which will not only change our nutrition for the better but lead to a longer and healthier life.

Alan N. Howard

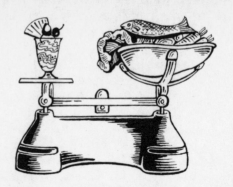

Weight Maintenance

'Many people who love to eat, constantly think about food – they daydream about places where mountains are made of fudge, rivers of flowing chocolate, and so on.'

Isaac Asimov – *The Science Fiction Weight-Loss Book*, 1983

Pitfalls of Weight Maintenance

Foodies are fascinated, delighted and comforted by food. They expect cuisine to be rich, compelling and delicious and they want portions to be generous. Even FFF's (formerly fat foodies) like me want food to conform to these standards. Although we long to stay slim we still crave plenty of good things to eat. I mean *really* good things. A leaf of lettuce, a naked morsel of broiled fish and a steamed vegetable do little to assuage our cravings. We want sauces, we want creamy textures, we want glamour, we even want, occasionally, junk food. What to do? Periods of abstinence followed by periods of indulgence are unhealthy and frustrating. Tiny portions of luscious things cause agony. Calorie counting and continuous deprivation in the name of slimness is sheer hell, and difficult as well. Yet a return to blimphood is too hideous to contemplate. Don't let this problem compromise your physical and mental health, *or* your sensual enjoyment of food. Be very careful. Don't fall into the three major weight maintenance traps.

'My soul is dark with stormy riot
Directly traceable to Diet.'

Samuel Hoffenstein – *Out of the Everywhere into the Here*, 1928

Trap #1 is Food Obsession

Food obsession occurs when one is constantly worried about what one eats, counts every Calorie, and checks the scale several times a day for added pounds. Pleasure in food becomes forbidden: feared and longed for at the same time. Occasional lapses occur. Fraught with guilt, the diner gorges on unsuitable, unhealthy and fattening foods, only to diet austerely for several days afterwards to make up for the digression. This behaviour results in an extremely unhealthy and nutritionally unbalanced diet and a dicey mental state.

Trap #2 is the Maths Major Syndrome

If you are determined to eat nutritious food, to balance your diet properly and to ingest every Calorie, every micro and macro nutrient in perfect harmony according to your needs, you may find yourself a slave to your calculator and to nutritional tables. Every meal becomes an intricate maths exercise as you work out protein levels, vitamins, minerals and trace minerals. . . . Mealtimes are grim accounting sessions, and soon become so boring that you fling your calculator away, and yourself into bad old eating habits again, in reaction to the tedium of endless calculations.

Trap #3 is the See-Saw Syndrome

I'm sure this is all too familiar to many of you. The initial joy and novelty of newly lost weight slowly wears off as food's siren song becomes louder and louder. It's so easy to fall back into the bad old habits. After all, if you eat that gooey chocolate-cream gateau, devour a jumbo order of greasy fish and chips, succumb to oceans of hollandaise, mountains of fudge, cream-slathered scones, why, you can always go back on your diet for a few days, can't you? Soon you find yourself eating mindlessly again, no thought at all for nutrition and Calories, until your clothes are embarrassingly tight and you can't stand the sight of your puffy face in the mirror any more. Then the struggle starts again to begin dieting, to stay on it through the first difficult days, to go through the exercise of dredging up the same old discipline and will-power. 'Losing weight on Cambridge is so easy,' you say, 'I did it once, I can always begin again tomorrow.' Sometimes tomorrow never comes, or it comes far too late. And if you *do* it again, lose the weight all over again, what happens? You're back to the maintenance point, face to face once more with those dreadful traps. It's a vicious circle!

Well – do I have the answer? Yes, of course I do. It's Slim Cuisine. I invented it, I live by it, I love it, and I want you to do the same. I believe in food that is scrumptious, glorious, fun to eat – but I also believe in a lifetime of good health and slimness. That's what Slim Cuisine is all about.

But do remember, accidents happen. If Christmas gets you, or Granny's Sunday lunch, or a trip to France, or a dinner out at an Indian restaurant, please don't give up in despair. All too often, such digressions become excuses to wallow in unsuitable food once more. Embrace the Cambridge Diet again with all your might. Then, when the danger of total regression has passed, continue to enrich your days with Slim Cuisine. But try not to make such accidents and recoveries a regular way of life or you'll find yourself right in the middle of the see-saw syndrome.

'Yet no sooner has a man achieved a one-pound loss,
Than he gains two through the application to an old familiar dish or
a new irresistible sauce.'

Ogden Nash – 'In the Diet Kitchen', 1929

Food As Comfort

'The further I travel in search of the ideal
slimming method, the more I am convinced that food is
one of the oldest and greatest comforters. If this
comforter – this secret return to the womb –
is suddenly taken away from me, I begin
to feel anxiety, depression, tension.'

Roy Andries de Groot – *Esquire* Magazine, 1972

During Cambridge sole source, daydreams of glorious food fill many waking moments. 'Soon, soon,' you promise yourself, 'I will reach my target weight, and then I can return to the comfort of real food.'

Comfort food encompasses a huge culinary spectrum. There are, of course, the rice puddings and creamy potato dishes of the nursery, but there are also the gorgeous sauces and rich desserts of classic cookery, the cold comfort of icecream, the steam-wreathed comfort of thick soups, and the nightmare-chasing solace of a post-midnight fridge forage. Unexpected contrasts of taste and texture give comfort too, as well as rustic, ethnic feasts and juvenile junk food like hamburgers, pizza and fried fish.

Alas, most of us separate the food that nourishes the soul from that which nourishes the body. We tend to indulge in comfort when we are deeply – psychically as well as physically – hungry, and then, in the name of slimness, return to spartan eating until the deep hunger strikes again. But why should this be? Why can't we nourish both body and soul at the same time?

This book is the result of my determination to achieve such double nourishment.

I want to eat food that satisfies in the deep recesses of the soul that only rich and delicious Comfort Food can reach, but I also regard a return to my old excessive weight with fear and trembling. It's foolish to compromise by dieting half the time and eating high-fat, high-Calorie disasters the other half. If you share my passions for slimness and health, and for Comfort Food, you can now indulge them both. The new techniques you will be using will change your life. For the first time in your adult life, you may find yourself enjoying your food body *and* soul, with none of the shadows of guilt or dissatisfaction that haunt so many of our mealtimes.

A Brief Overview of Slim Cuisine Basics

Yes, there is culinary life after achieving your target weight. A culinary life that does not result in a depressing and unhealthy regain of all your lost poundage. The new techniques described in this book will enable you to produce rich, satisfying and comforting food without the excess Calories and fat. All Slim Cuisine recipes are nutrient dense, Calorie shy and exceedingly palatable. Here is a brief overview of the basic rules.

'Poor old Pyecraft! Great, uneasy jelly of substance! The fattest clubman in London. He sits at one of the little club tables in the huge bay of the fire, stuffing. What is he stuffing? I glance judiciously, and catch him biting at a round of hot buttered teacake.'

H. G. Wells – *The Truth About Pyecraft*, 1928

1. Except for seasoning your non-stick cookware (see page 47) dispense with all cooking fats and oils. It doesn't matter if the fats are unsaturated (monounsaturated or polyunsaturated) or saturated; dump them all, and forget about them for the rest of your life. The no-no list includes:
** Butter
** Margarine
** Drippings, lard, suet, poultry fats
** Poultry skin
** All oils: sunflower, olive, peanut, corn, soybean, etc.
** Solid, hydrogenated shortenings
** Mayonnaise and salad dressings

** All dairy products *not* made from skimmed milk with the exception of a few medium fat cheeses: Parmesan, semi-skimmed Mozzarella, Bruder Basil, Jarlsberg, medium fat chevres (French goat cheeses), which may be used occasionally in small quantities.
** High-fat meats
** Nuts, except for a very small amount here and there for flavouring and garnishing.
** Whole eggs only *very* occasionally. The yolk is quite high in fat. The whites, on the other hand, are fat free; use them as often as you please.
** Baked goods and prepared foods containing any of the above fats, or high-fat ingredients
'Stop!' I hear you cry. 'How can I manage to cook anything even vaguely delicious, hampered by such rules?' Read on.
2. Use the following as substitutes for the forbidden fats:
** Skimmed milk yoghurt. Use it as is or drain it to make a substitute for cream cheese or a base for Slim mayonnaise and salad dressings. (See page 27.)
** Skimmed milk fromage blanc or fromage frais. Use as described for yoghurt, above, also in place of soured cream and creme fraiche.
** Buttermilk cultured from skimmed milk
** Skimmed milk quark
** Skimmed milk and skimmed milk powder
** Chicken, beef and vegetable stocks. (See page 35.) Use very good quality stock in place of butter and oil to sauté-flavour vegetables. (See page 22.)
** *Lean* meats, poultry trimmed of skin and fat

'Things are seldom what they seem,
Skimmed milk masquerades as cream.'

W. S. Gilbert – *H.M.S. Pinafore*, 1878

3. Use vegetables that have been baked and then puréed to give body to sauces, casseroles, stews, soups and gratins. (See pages 29 to 33.) The best vegetables for this purpose are garlic, onions, carrots, potatoes, parsnips, swedes and turnips.
4. Use baked, puréed aubergine as a filler in meatballs, hamburgers, and bolognese sauce. It gives body and moisture, cuts down on the amount of meat used and adds *no* aubergine taste. Purée grilled and peeled peppers, season and use as a no-fat, delicious sauce for pasta, meats, fish or poultry.

19

5. Don't give up desserts, only those that are laden with fat and excessive sugar. For instance, icecream, that high-fat, sugary disaster, becomes low-fat, low calorie and highly nutritious made the Slim Cuisine way. (See page 203.)

Fat-Soluble Vitamins

Three of the essential vitamins (A, D and E), the 'fat-soluble' vitamins, are normally found in the fatty substances we eat. A price that we might pay for the reduction in fat would be a reduction in the available food sources of these vitamins. Vitamin A, however, can be made in our body from substances called carotenes that are found in non-fatty vegetables (rich sources are green and yellow vegetables such as carrots, spinach, tomatoes, peppers, sprouts and fruits such as apricots). If your meals include these lovely foods, then ample vitamin A will be provided. Vitamin E is less readily available but fortunately our needs for this vitamin are tied strongly to the amount of unsaturated fat we take in. As we will be dramatically reducing our fat intake we need proportionately less of the vitamin. Wholegrain cereals are rich sources of vitamin E and considerable quantities can also be obtained from leafy green vegetables, meat and egg yolk, all available in Slim Cuisine recipes.

Vitamin D presents a special problem. Most of the world derive adequate amounts of vitamin D through the skin's exposure to sunlight. In some countries, all dairy products are irradiated with ultra violet light to produce a fortification with vitamin D and ensure that people receive adequate amounts. Sun-starved countries, such as Great Britain, need additional amounts of vitamin D. In Great Britain, margarines are fortified with vitamin D. A restriction in dietary fats will make this one major source unavailable and could result in inadequate intake of the vitamin regardless of other foods consumed. The sad fact, however, is that it is necessary to eat over 1200 Calories of margarine each day or 9000 Calories of butter to get our daily requirement of 10 micrograms of vitamin D. Supplements of fat-soluble vitamins which include vitamin D are so readily available that it would be wise for people in sun-starved areas to insure against nutritional deficiency, regardless of their food preferences. You can take 10 micrograms daily or 70 micrograms weekly in tablet form. A word of caution, however. Fat-soluble vitamins such as vitamin D can become toxic if eaten in too large a quantity, so just make sure your dose does not exceed an average of 10 micrograms a day. If your vitamin D supplement also contains vitamins A and E, your fat-soluble vitamin insurance will be complete.

'The hour of grim decision is the first Monday after the New Year of any year. And this day should have a name: All Fat Soul's Day, maybe.'
Miriam Ungerer – *Country Food*, 1983

Techniques

'A diet's a very delicate thing.
You have to keep your momentum going.
You have to stick to your routine.'

Ellen Gilchrist, *Victory Over Japan*, 1984

Some Slim Cuisine techniques – the ones you will use over and over again – are detailed in this section. Other more specific techniques – stir-frying without oil, for instance, or ridding meat of fat – are outlined in the appropriate chapters.

I hope that these techniques will enable you to think about cookery in an entirely new way. Make them part of your culinary life, substitute them for the old high-fat methods, and you will be cutting hundreds, even thousands of Calories out of your day's intake. One of the most exciting results of this kitchen revolution is that you will be able to increase the *amount* of food you ingest each day. Small portions of delicious things cause anguish. With these new techniques, food will still be delicious and you can enjoy large, satisfying portions. Your total nutrition intake will be high, but fat and Calories will be low.

Use these techniques to your own taste. Once they are mastered, adapt them to your own recipes; recipes that please you and those you feed.

Sautéing In Stock

Think about the way many recipes begin: 'Sauté onions and/or garlic in 4 (or more) tablespoons oil or butter.' Follow such directions and immediately, without even thinking, you add at least 400 fat-Calories to the meal. Of course, it is usually much more than 400. Other recipes in the same meal may begin with similar directions. Add to this the recipes prepared for the other meals of the day – butter or margarine spread on bread, fried foods, high-fat snacks, melted butter on vegetables, mayonnaise on sandwiches, etc. etc. – and the day's fat-Calories intake can easily mount to well over 1,000, without any effort at all. Begin your Slim Cuisine kitchen revolution by changing the sauté method from a fat-based one to a stock-based one.

It is important to realize that merely boiling or simmering onions in stock result in *flabby* vegetables, not *sautéed* vegetables. My technique combines onions and/or other vegetables with stock in a way that achieves a true, deeply flavoured *sauté* effect.

SAUTÉED ONIONS

61 Calories per 1 large sautéed onion
0.2 g fat
(traditional sautéed onions: 250 Calories per 1 large sautéed onion, 24 g fat)

This is the basic technique. Chopped carrots and celery can be added. The best pot to use is an 8-in/20-cm enamelled cast-iron frying pan. Do *not* use a non-stick frying pan. The intense flavour that results from this method depends upon a little judicious and controlled burning, occurring toward the end of the recipe. Don't even think about substituting a bouillon cube for homemade stock. The cube is loaded with salt, monosodium glutamate and other undesirables and has no place in Slim Cuisine. (See page 37 for recipes for and hints about stock.)

---

1 large onion, chopped	*Splash of dry vermouth, dry red or*
1 clove garlic, minced	*white wine, dry sherry, wine*
6 fl oz/180 ml stock	*vinegar or additional stock*

---

1   Combine all ingredients except the final splash in an 8-in/20-cm frying pan. Cover and bring to a boil.
2   Uncover. Boil for approximately 5 minutes until most of the liquid has cooked away. Reduce heat and simmer until just about dry and beginning to stick a little bit.

3   Lower the heat. Toss and stir constantly with a wooden spoon until you smell a lovely, toasty, oniony aroma and the bottom of the pan is beginning to brown just a bit. Pour in a splash of dry wine or additional stock and turn the heat up again. Stir with the wooden spoon, scraping up all the browned bits. When the liquid is gone, the onions should be meltingly tender and amber-coloured and the tantalizing smell should be driving all members of the household mad. Remove from heat. Use in a recipe at once or refrigerate for later use.

BROWNED ONIONS

Makes about ¾ pt/450 ml
351 Calories per recipe
0.9 g fat
(traditional browned onions: 851 Calories per recipe, 40 g fat)

This makes the most delicious concoction imaginable. It is what the French call onion jam or onion marmalade. This Slim Cuisine version can save you many Calories, yet the final result is just as good as the sinful versions, if not more so.

---

6 large onions, peeled and trimmed	*Splash of additional stock, dry*
16 fl oz/480 ml stock	*vermouth, dry red or white*
	wine, dry sherry or wine vinegar

---

1   Cut onions in half. Slice into thin half-moons. Combine onions and 16 fl oz/480 ml of stock in a deep, 10-inch/25-cm, enamelled cast-iron frying pan. Cover and bring to a boil. Reduce heat a bit and simmer briskly for 10 minutes.
2   Uncover. Simmer for 35–40 minutes, stirring occasionally. After this period of time the onions will be turning amber brown and the liquid will be almost gone. Stir constantly and allow to cook for a few more minutes. The onions will begin to stick just a bit. Keep stirring for approximately 10 minutes more until the onions are just about dry and browned deposits are forming on the bottom of the frying pan. As you stir with your wooden spoon, keep scraping up the browned deposits.
3   Turn up the heat a tiny bit and let the onions start to burn just a *little* – that's what makes the ravishing flavour. Be very careful not to allow wholesale burning and blackening – that way lies ruin.
4   Splash in 3–4 tablespoons of dry wine, wine vinegar or additional stock. Boil until just about dry, vigorously stirring and scraping up the browned bits on the bottom of the frying pan.

Immediately remove from heat. Use a rubber spatula to scrape the mass of browned onions into a storage container. Use as a garnish for lean meats, use as a base for stews, sauces and soups, or serve as a vegetable accompaniment.

'One of the most satisfying properties of the onion . . . is its grace . . . in bringing out the flavour of anything with which it is combined.'

Jean Bothwell, *Onions Without Tears*, 1951

ONION-HERB INFUSION

81 Calories per recipe
0 g fat

This is another way of using onions and stock (spring onions or shallots this time) to make an intensely flavoured base for many recipes. Please note that in this method and the previous one the wine is boiled dry so no alcohol (and no alcohol Calories) are left. The herb you choose for the infusion will depend upon how you wish to use it. Tarragon, oregano, thyme all work beautifully with this method.

½ pt/300 ml sliced spring onions (both the green and white portions), or finely chopped shallots or finely chopped onion	Pinch or two cayenne pepper (to taste)
4 fl oz/120 ml stock	2½ tablespoons chopped fresh herbs or ½ tablespoon dried herbs
4 fl oz/120 ml dry vermouth or dry red or white wine	1 tablespoon chopped fresh parsley

---

Combine all ingredients in a small, heavy frying pan. Bring to a boil, reduce heat and simmer briskly, uncovered, until almost all the liquid has evaporated. Use at once in a recipe or refrigerate for later use.

SAUTÉED ONIONS FOR CURRIES

175 Calories per recipe
0.5 g fat

Curries present a challenge. Indian cookery depends very heavily on ghee (clarified butter) or oil. The myriad spices and herbs that make up the flavouring mix for each curry must be gently cooked in the fat or oil. Sometimes herbs or spices are whole, sometimes ground, or sometimes pounded to a paste with garlic, ginger and onions, but in whatever form they are always gently fried early in the recipe. It is this important step that gives Indian food its distinctive taste and texture. Just adding the appropriate spice mix to a fatless version of the recipe results in a finished dish with a sandy, gritty texture and a harsh, raw-spice taste: unpleasant to eat, and very un-Indian as well. Frying the spices dry in a non-stick pan scorches them. I've finally worked out a way to 'fry' the spices with onions, ginger and garlic in such a way that produces a smooth, gentle effect, with no scorching, and in which all the seasonings blend well, and leave no harshness. As is typical in Indian cookery, each curry recipe in this book has its own spice mix. The sauce base that results from this technique can be used to make meat, poultry, fish or vegetable curries.

---

3 onions, chopped, sliced or cut into eighths
10 fl oz/300 ml stock

Spice mixture (see individual curry recipes for specifics)

---

1   Separate the segments of the chopped onion pieces and spread them in a heavy, non-stick frying pan. Add *no* liquid or fat. Heat the frying pan gently. Cook at moderate heat, without stirring, for 7–10 minutes, until the onions are sizzling, speckled with dark amber, and beginning to stick to the pan.
2   Stir in 10 fl oz/300 ml of stock and let it bubble up, stirring up the browned deposits in the pan with a wooden spoon as it bubbles. Stir in the spices and garlic. Turn the heat down a bit and simmer, stirring frequently, until the mixture is very thick (not at all soupy), and the onions and spices are 'frying' in their own juices. Don't rush this step, it is essential that the spices should not have a raw harsh taste. Taste. Cook very gently for a few more minutes if necessary.
3   If you wish, for a thick sauce, purée half of the mixture in a liquidizer or food processor, then combine the puréed mixture with the unpuréed portion.

To this basic onion-curry mixture add more stock, or chopped tomatoes, or tomato paste. Stir in cubed meat, poultry, vegetables, prawns or fish and simmer until done. At the very end, yoghurt may be added to the sauce. (See index for specific curry recipes.)

Note: This basic method is correct for chilli con carne, goulashes and other dishes made with paprika, as well as curry.

'Reading them [Indian cookery books] is a great adventure: Roast this or that mystery spice for 1.75 minutes, grind it to ½ mm pieces, fry for 17 seconds in jumping-bean fat at 316° F then add it to another mystery spice. Soak in hokum-cokum water for 2 days then blanch in the midday sun at 81° F.'

Pat Chapman, *Indian Restaurant Cookbook*, 1984

SWEET AND SOUR ONIONS

67 Calories per onion
0.16 g fat

These rich onions are perfect as a topping for meats – braised liver, grilled steak, hamburgers etc. – but they are very good on their own as well. (See page 88 for the lowest-fat steaks.)

---

6 large onions, peeled	*1 tablespoon sugar*
4 fl oz/120 ml stock	*2 cloves garlic, crushed*
½ teaspoon Dijon mustard	*1 dried bay leaf, broken in half*
1½ tablespoons red wine vinegar	*Salt to taste*

---

1   Slice onion into ½ in/1.3 cm thick rings. Place in a non-reactive frying pan with the remaining ingredients.
2   Bring to a boil, reduce heat, cover and simmer for 30 minutes, uncovering to stir occasionally.
3   Remove the cover and simmer, stirring until the onions are beautifully browned and the liquid has greatly reduced. Remove bay leaf before serving.

SAUTÉED MUSHROOMS

60 Calories per recipe
1 g fat
(traditional sautéed mushrooms: 210 Calories, 22 g fat)

I didn't think I would be able to produce acceptable 'sautéed' mushrooms without butter or, at the very least, a bit of oil. I was wrong. These mushrooms are not only good – they are addictive. Use them as a garnish, stir them into soups and sauces, or eat them right out of the pan, if you are as wild about mushrooms as I am.

½ pound/225 g mushrooms,	*4 fl oz/120 ml chicken or vegetable*
cleaned and quartered	*stock*
4 fl oz/120 ml medium dry red wine	*Dash or two soy sauce*
	Freshly ground pepper to taste

---

1   Put the mushrooms and liquid into a non-reactive, non-stick heavy frying pan. Stir to combine everything very well.
2   Simmer, stirring occasionally. First the mushrooms will release a good deal of extra liquid. Continue simmering, stirring occasionally until the liquid is almost gone. Let the mushrooms 'fry' gently in their own juices for a few moments. Do not let them scorch or stick. Season to taste and serve, or refrigerate for a later use.

'But yesterday I caught him in her dairy, eating fresh butter with a tablespoon. Today he is not well.'

W. S. Gilbert, *Patience*, 1881

DRAINING YOGHURT OR FROMAGE FRAIS TO MAKE CREAM CHEESE AND MAYONNAISE

111 Calories per 3½ oz/100 g (yoghurt cream cheese)
0.6 g fat
154 Calories per 3½ oz/100 g (fromage frais cream cheese)
0.4 g fat

This 'cream' cheese is thick and creamy, perfect for spreading on bread or toast or dolloping into jacket potatoes in place of high-fat soured cream, cream cheese or butter. Use it, too, as a base for 'mayonnaise' or creamy salad dressing. Yoghurt cheese and fromage frais cheese are very easy to make and so versatile that it pays to have some on hand in the fridge at all times. Fromage frais results in a milder cheese than yoghurt.

1   Line a sieve or colander with a long piece of doubled damp cheesecloth. (Rinse it first in cold water, then wring it out well.) Place the lined sieve over a large bowl. Dump in the yoghurt or fromage frais, fold the cheesecloth over to cover well and leave in a cool part of the kitchen for 24 hours. Every once in a while, pour off the liquid that accumulates in the bowl.
2   At the end of the 24-hour period unwrap the cheese and scrape it into a bowl or crock. Refrigerate. If desired, interesting ingredients can be added to the cheese to produce a delicious spread. Try one of these:

Crushed garlic marinated in wine vinegar	Shredded smoked fish
Chopped fresh chives	Minced, mixed vegetables (radishes, celery, carrots, red and yellow peppers)
Chopped fresh dill	

MAYONNAISE

Makes approximately ⅖ pt/240 ml

Forget real mayonnaise, yummy though it may be. The wicked stuff is made from egg yolks and a whole lot of oil, with a little mustard and wine vinegar thrown in. Pure, unadulterated fat, with no redeeming value whatsoever. Slim Cuisine 'mayonnaise' is low-fat and low-Calorie. Use it in salad recipes or as a sandwich spread. (See the Salad chapter for more ideas.) You may feel as smug as you please as you eat your salad and sandwiches: real mayo has 99 Calories and 11 grams of fat per tablespoon; this version only 7 Calories, and 0.03 grams of fat.

⅕ pt/120 ml yoghurt cheese or fromage frais cheese, or a combination	3–4 tablespoons buttermilk
	1–2 tablespoons wine vinegar
1–2 teaspoons Dijon mustard (to taste)	Salt and freshly ground pepper to taste

Whisk all the ingredients together, adding the buttermilk and vinegar gradually, tasting as you go, until a mayonnaise-like consistency is achieved, and until the flavour pleases you. Season to taste. Refrigerate overnight for flavours to blend.

Note: Add any one of the following to your mayonnaise, if desired:

Crushed garlic	Red pepper purée (see page 32)
Chilli powder, hot or mild	Tomato paste
Hungarian paprika, hot or mild	Chopped fresh herbs
Curry spices	

'Mayonnaise: One of the sauces which serve the French in place of a State Religion.'

Ambrose Bierce, *The Devil's Dictionary*, 1925

STABILIZED YOGHURT

295 Calories per recipe
0 g fat

Heat applied to yoghurt causes it to curdle. Very low-fat yoghurt seems to be more prone to curdling than that with higher fat levels. Cornflour stabilizes the yoghurt so that it can be used in soups and hot sauces, but even stabilized yoghurt must be simmered only gently. Boiling will cause it to 'break' or become grainy.

---

2 teaspoons cornflour blended with 1 tablespoon water	*1 pt/600 ml skimmed milk yoghurt at room temperature*

---

1   Whisk together the cornflour, water and yoghurt. Dump into a non-reactive, heavy saucepan. Gently bring to a simmer, stirring.
2   Simmer gently for 5 minutes, stirring often.

Baked Vegetables

Everyone knows that potatoes can be baked with delicious effect. But did you ever think of baking a whole head of garlic? (Yes, I said garlic!) or a large sweet onion? It can be done, and the results will delight you, both for immediate eating and for use in thickening soups, stews and sauces.

'Garlic is as good as ten mothers.'

Teluga proverb

BAKED GARLIC

21 Calories per head of garlic
0 g fat

When garlic bakes in the oven for an hour or so, it loses its strong assertiveness and becomes mellow, sweet and vaguely nut-like. The texture changes too; the meat of each clove softens into a purée. The purée is excellent as a thickening agent for soups, sauces and stews. It imparts body and a mysterious and gentle flavour boost without adding salt, fat or excess Calories. The whole baked heads of garlic also make a dandy starter for a dinner party. It is fun to watch each guest fidget nervously in their chairs as you

29

place the garlic in front of them. 'A garlic allergy, perhaps?', they desperately think. 'A mad dash home to check on the children?' Quickly demonstrate the proper method of spreading the garlic on toast and take a bite yourself. When your guests see that you survive that first taste, they will be emboldened to try. And once they have had that first taste, they will be garlic fans for life. Be sure to use the largest, firmest, freshest heads of garlic you can find for this procedure.

Whole heads of garlic
Toasted rounds of wholemeal bread

---

1   Preheat oven to 375° F (190° C/Gas Mark 4).
2   Remove the papery outer covering of the whole garlic heads, but do not separate the cloves or peel them. Place as many whole heads of garlic on a large square of foil (shiny side of the foil in) as there are people to be served. Fold up the foil so that the cloves are completely wrapped.
3   Bake in a preheated oven for approximately 1 hour 15 minutes (depending upon size of garlic bulb).
4   Serve each diner a head of garlic and some bread. Separate the cloves. Hold a clove over a piece of bread and squeeze. The garlic purée will pop out, like toothpaste from a tube.

GARLIC PURÉE

Keep a supply of this lovely stuff in the refrigerator and use it to liven up all kinds of dishes. Stir it into soups and stews by the spoonful; use it to thicken sauces, and to spread on bread (mixed with quark or Slim Cuisine cream cheese if you wish). Garlic popcorn – freshly popped popcorn with a good dollop of garlic purée – makes a simple, unbelievably savoury snack. No salt is needed; the garlic flavour is sufficient.

1   To make a batch of garlic purée for later use, let baked heads of garlic (preceding recipe) cool, unwrapped, for at least 5 minutes.
2   Gently separate the cloves and squeeze each one over a fine-meshed sieve so that the softened garlic pops into the sieve.
3   With a wooden spatula or spoon rub the garlic through the sieve into a small container or bowl.
4   Cover tightly with plastic wrap and refrigerate until the purée is needed.

QUICK PURÉE

If you are in a hurry, you may skip the sieve. Simply squeeze the cloves, one by one, over a bowl. When they have all been squeezed, use a rubber spatula to push the purée into a neat mound, cover tightly with plastic wrap and refrigerate until needed.

'Some people are allergic to garlic. They may or may not be vampires.'

Lloyd John Harris, *The Garlic Lover's Handbook*, 1986

BAKED ONION

57 Calories per onion

A baked onion served whole, sprinkled with fresh pepper and lemon juice, makes a lovely vegetable accompaniment to a meal. It can also be puréed in a liquidizer and used as garlic purée can be used: to thicken sauces, soups and stews and to give them a low-fat, low-Calorie and low-salt flavour and texture boost.

Large Spanish onions

---

1   Preheat the oven to 425° F (220° C/Gas Mark 6).
2   Put the onions on a double sheet of foil, shiny side out, but do not wrap them. Bake for 1¼ hours, or until very soft and almost collapsed.
3   With a sharp knife, cut off the stem and root ends of the onions. Remove and discard the blackened skin and first layer. Serve as they are with pepper and lemon juice, or put the onions into a liquidizer and purée for use in other recipes.

BAKED OR GRILLED PEPPERS

22 Calories per pepper

Both yellow and red bell peppers (capsicums) have an enticing fleshy sweetness. When baked or grilled the skin chars. Peel off that blackened skin, and the meat of the pepper is revealed; jewel bright, tender and splendidly flavourful. The baked pepper can be cut into strips, sprinkled with wine vinegar and served as vegetable; or puréed and served as a sauce or a garnish. Delicious juices will accumulate in the baking pan as the peppers cook. More will accumulate in the container in which the peppers are stored. Save these juices for sauces and salad dressing.

Red and yellow bell peppers (capsicums). (Green peppers   *may be used too, but they are not as pretty, or as sweet)*

---

1 Preheat oven to 425° F (220° C/Gas Mark 6). Place peppers on a foil-lined sheet (shiny side out).
2 Bake for 1–1¼ hours, turning the peppers with tongs 2–3 times during the baking. They will blacken and char.
3 Enclose the hot peppers in a paper bag, and leave for 10 minutes. Steam will form between the charred skin and the flesh, making peeling much easier.
4 With your fingers, strip off the charred skin and discard it. Discard the seeds and the stem. Refrigerate as they are, or purée in the liquidizer and refrigerate. The peppers will keep in the refrigerator for a week. The purée can be frozen.

Note: If you have a gas cooker, to roast the peppers place them directly on the flame of the plate on the gas stove. As the peppers blacken and char, turn them with tongs. Or they may be cut in half and grilled, cut side down, until they blacken and char. When blackened and charred, continue with Steps 3 and 4, as above. Both these methods are quicker than the oven one.

BAKED AUBERGINE

42 Calories per aubergine
0.3 g fat

The chopped flesh of a baked aubergine is a wonderful filler for hamburgers and meatballs. It adds moistness and lightness, and cuts the Calories without adding any taste of its own. Even if you hate aubergine, you will love what it does to minced meat. For a delicious Middle Eastern dip, try the baked flesh, puréed or mashed with baked garlic, baked onion and baked pepper purées, yoghurt, chopped tomatoes, herbs and spices (cumin, coriander leaves, cayenne). Serve with pitta bread triangles, or crudités (raw vegetable dippers).

Serve creamy tuna mousse (page 56) with crisp curls of homemade wholemeal Melba toast.

32

1   Preheat oven to 400° F (200° C/Gas Mark 7).
2   Pierce the aubergines in several places with a fork or thin
     skewer. Bake directly on the oven rack for 30–40 minutes, until
     soft and collapsed. Cool.
3   Cut away the stem, strip off the skins, and chop or mash.
     (If the clumps of seeds are large and tough they may be
     discarded.)

BAKED TURNIPS, CARROTS AND PARSNIPS

25 Calories per medium turnip
0.2 g fat
64 Calories per medium parsnip
0.4 g fat
45 Calories per medium carrot
0.2 g fat

Why condemn turnips, carrots and parsnips to a watery, vitamin-
stripped death? Forget boiling. Bake them so that they steam in
their own juices. Instead of poor flabby things, they will be tender
and succulent. When mashed or puréed, these baked vegetables
are very useful for thickening and giving body to soups and stews.
They may also be eaten as they are, or mashed with a bit of
buttermilk and Parmesan cheese. Or they may be baked into a
crusty gratin (See pages 158–9).

| *Turnips* | *Carrots* |
| *Parsnips* | |

1   Preheat the oven to 425° F (220° C/Gas Mark 6).
2   Peel the turnips. Scrub the carrots and parsnips. Leave them
     unpeeled if they are to be eaten whole, peel them if they are to
     be mashed.
3   Wrap the turnips loosely in foil, shiny side in. Crimp well so
     that no steam escapes. Do the same with the parsnips and the
     carrots. Bake for 1–1¼ hours, until tender.

A vivid bean soup (page 67) begins a meal with panache.
Jellied gazpacho is lovely unmoulded onto a buttermilk pool.

Adapting Recipes

The comforting thing about Slim Cuisine is the flexibility it gives to your everyday cooking. You can use many of your old recipes; in fact you can try new ones from intriguing new cookbooks. Just apply Slim Cuisine techniques in place of traditional ones and you will be safe from the fat demons that lurk in conventional cookery. If a recipe calls for onions sautéed in butter or oil for instance, substitute Slim Cuisine sautéed onions. Use baked garlic purée instead of minced garlic sautéed in oil, fromage frais or yoghurt cheese in place of sweet or sour cream, Slim Cuisine 'mayonnaise' in place of the very wicked real thing. You will save thousands of Calories, yet eating and exploring the world of cuisine will continue to be a joyous activity.

Ingredients

'[Maria Callas's] close friend Marlene Dietrich
feared that the loss of weight might have weakened her,
and, becoming anxious during the rehearsals,
spent several hours boiling down eight pounds of
the best beef to a quart of the very finest broth.
"It's wonderful!" Maria declared. "How kind! Do tell me –
what brand of beef cubes did you use?"'

Charles Neilson Gattey, *Foie Gras and Trumpets*, 1984

Stock

Stock is vital to Slim Cuisine. If the quality of your stock is high, so
will be the quality of your food. Avoid bouillon cubes and powders
that are laden with salt and monosodium glutamate.

BASIC CHICKEN STOCK

This is very simple to make, but it does take time. The recipe can be
multiplied and it freezes beautifully, so set aside a leisurely evening or slow Saturday to make a huge batch. Freeze it in small
containers, and then pull one out as needed. An easy way to make
the stock is to keep simmering the chicken in the liquid for the full
cooking time until it completely falls apart. If you are using a whole
chicken do not succumb to this method. Yes, the stock will be very

full bodied, but the chicken will have cooked to rags, and be good for nothing but the cat. Far better to remove the chicken when it is tender and succulent and can be used in any number of delicious dishes. Use its bones to finish the stock. Boiling hens are almost impossible to find these days, so a roasting chicken is what you will need for this recipe. For best results, use a free-range chicken. Of course, if you wish you may use just wings, necks and backs, or even chicken carcasses that you have saved in the freezer. If you use these scraps, simmer them until they have given their all to the broth. There is no need to go through the cooling, and boning process described in Steps 2 and 3. Homemade stock, meticulously strained and skimmed, contains negligible calories. Makes approximately 2 quarts

1 2½–3½ lb/1,125 g dressed chicken, or chicken wings, backs and necks	2 carrots
	1 small onion
	1 garlic clove, unpeeled
3 celery stalks	Several sprigs of parsley
2 parsnips	Salt

1   Wash the chicken well inside and out and pull off excess fat. Scrub the celery, parsnips and carrots, leaving the carrots and parsnips unpeeled. Peel the onion. Cut the celery, carrots, parsnips and onion into chunks.

2   Boil the chicken and any extra chicken parts in 6½ pts/3,900 ml of water. After 10 minutes, skim all foam and scum from the top. Add the garlic and vegetables. Reduce the heat so that the liquid stays at a steady simmer. Simmer, partially covered, until the chicken is tender and succulent, about 50–60 minutes. Let the chicken cool in the partially covered pot for no less than 1 hour, but no more than 2 hours. If you are using backs, necks, wings and carcasses just let it simmer for another ½ to 1 hour, and then proceed to Step 4.

3   Carefully remove the whole chicken from the pot. (It will still be quite warm, so be careful.) Pull the chicken from the bones and tear it into chunks. Discard the skin and all bits of fat and gristle. Place the meat in a wide, shallow container, moisten with a bit of the stock, cover well and refrigerate immediately for use in a later recipe. Return all bones to the stock. Bring to a boil, reduce heat and simmer, partially covered, for another ½ hour.

4   Season with a bit of salt. Carefully strain the stock through a fine sieve or strainer. Press down on the solids to extract all their goodness. Pour the stock into clean jars, cover tightly and refrigerate overnight.

5   By the next day the fat will have risen to the top of each jar of
    stock and solidified. Meticulously scrape away every speck of
    fat and discard it. The stock itself may have jelled. Don't
    worry, this is just a sign that you have made a good, gelatine-
    rich broth. It will liquefy again when heated. Pour the defatted
    stock into freezer containers and store in the freezer until
    needed.

Simple Stock

I have racked my brains and ransacked the groceries, health-food
shops and delicatessens for a quick substitute for homemade stock.
Here are two thoughts for cooks in a hurry.

1   Most Chinese take-aways and restaurants have huge quanti-
    ties of good quality chicken stock on hand. In many cases, salt
    and monosodium glutamate are not added until the moment
    the stock is transformed into a soup or added to a cooked dish.
    If you are a regular customer at a friendly local take-away, ask
    the owner if you can occasionally buy some. Often, if you
    bring a container, the proprietors of many such places (if they
    know you) will cheerfully fill it for a very modest price. When
    you get the stock home, it needs to be chilled so that the fat can
    be skimmed off. Quick chill, if necessary by placing the stock
    in the freezer for a few minutes or by dropping a few ice cubes
    into the stock.
2   There are vegetable stock cubes and vegetable bouillon pastes
    available but most of the ones I have tried taste perfectly awful,
    and will ruin any recipe you add them to. Marigold, however,
    makes a palatable vegetable bouillon powder that is available
    from some delicatessens and health-food shops.

VEGETABLE STOCK

Vegetable stock is quicker, easier and less expensive than chicken
stock. There are many versions, one of which follows. Vegetable
stock is a boon for vegetarians, orthodox Jews who want to cook
with stock for a dairy meal, or for anyone else who for one reason or
another does not want a meaty stock. Again, as with chicken stock,
make it in large quantities and freeze it in small containers or in ice
cube bags or trays.

4 leeks	2–3 fresh bay leaves or one dried
5 sticks of celery with leaves	bay leaf
2 large onions	3–4 sprigs fresh thyme
4 oz/112 g mushrooms	Handful of fresh parsley
4 white turnips	1 large potato
5 carrots	Salt and freshly ground pepper
4 parsnips	

1   Trim the vegetables and clean them well, but leave them unpeeled. Cut them into large chunks. Place them in a deep pot and cover generously with cold water. Bring to the boil.
2   Skim off foam. Partially cover the pot. Lower the heat and simmer for approximately 1 hour.
3   Season with just a bit of salt and some freshly ground pepper. Strain the broth through a fine sieve or strainer (discard the solids). Cool and refrigerate. Use the stock within 3 days or store in the freezer.

SMOKED CHICKEN

There are very good smoked chickens available in some speciality shops and delicatessens. I regularly buy the Galina brand from Greenstage in Newmarket, producers of the famous Musk's Sausage. A smoked chicken is ready to eat so needs no further cooking other than a brief warming, but it's good cold too. It can be stored in the freezer for months, with no appreciable loss of quality. Use smoked chicken in sandwiches (for suggestions see page 194) or to give a wonderful smoky accent to pasta dishes (see page 149 for an example). If you can, freeze your smoked chicken in pieces, because you will only need a little bit at a time. *Never* throw away the smoked chicken bones and scraps. Save them in the freezer until you have enough to make stock. The stock will have a haunting and lovely smoky edge, making it perfect for split pea and bean soups, chestnut soup, some sauces – anywhere you want a smoky taste without resorting to high-fat smoked bacon, ham and so on.

Dairy Products

QUARK

A German moist, soft spreadable, white curd cheese. It can be purchased with three different fat contents; less than 1 per cent, 20 per cent and 40 per cent. Of course, you will grab the lowest and pass the others by without a qualm. I like quark spread on bread in place of butter. Its bland creaminess makes it perfect for use in recipes that call for cream cheese, soured cream or even whipped cream. Quark can also be used for cooking in many sauces that call for cream. 3½ oz/100 g of the versatile stuff contains 77 Calories.

SKIMMED MILK YOGHURT

Yoghurt is an extremely valuable and useful product (3½ oz/100 g is 55 Calories, 0.2 g fat). Use it in place of soured cream and cream fraiche (3½ oz/100 g is 212 Calories, 20 g fat). Or drain it to form a delightful cream cheese (see page 27). Yoghurt cream cheese can be turned into a fat-free, low-Calorie mayonnaise (see page 28).

Undrained yoghurt can also be used in cooking in place of cream. If the yoghurt is to be simmered in a sauce or cooked dish, it must be stabilized to prevent curdling (see page 29).

The Magic of Yoghurt

Ilya Metchnikoff was obsessed with *Lactobacillus Bulgaris*. Metchnikoff, a Nobel Laureate and the sub-director of the Pasteur Institute in Paris, believed the human ageing process to be tragic and premature. He was convinced that a regular diet of yoghurt (the result of the bacteria *Lactobacillus Bulgaris* on milk) would significantly prolong life, and hold senility and physical degeneration at bay. Secure in his belief, Metchnikoff wrote a book, *The Prolongation of Life*, and fed himself lavish amounts of yoghurt until the end of his life. That end, alas, came at the age of 71 – a decent enough span, but not the century-plus length of years he was so sure he would achieve.

Today, almost seventy years after the publication of Metchnikoff's book, yoghurt is a supermarket staple. Although it won't help you to live forever, it is a magnificent cooking ingredient – tangy, custardy and smooth – and the low-fat version is one of the standbys of Slim Cuisine. Thank you, Monsieur Metchnikoff: how lovely it is to indulge in mayonnaise and creamy salad dressings without indulging in fat and excess Calories as well.

BUTTERMILK

Cultured from skimmed milk, buttermilk is thick, creamy, only slightly tangy and a mere 35 Calories per 3½ oz/100 g, 0.1 g fat. It gives a lovely flavour and texture to sweets and to low fat 'mayonnaise'-type salad dressings. It is worth searching for. Many

39

large supermarkets carry buttermilk, as do many small deli-catessens and whole food shops. Strawberries, buttermilk and a light sprinkling of brown sugar make a heavenly finish to a meal. Buttermilk is also an important component of Slim Cuisine ice-creams (see page 203).

FROMAGE BLANC/FROMAGE FRAIS

There are several different brands available in supermarkets throughout the country. Make sure you are buying a fromage blanc that contains less than 1 per cent fat. Fromage blanc is amazingly like soured cream and creme fraiche in taste and texture, but it contains only 44 Calories per 3½ oz/100 g, 0.1 g fat. Soured cream and creme fraiche contain 18 per cent fat and 212 Calories, 20 g fat per 3½ oz/100 g. Use fromage blanc in sauces, jacket potatoes, sweets and anywhere else you would use soured cream. Like sour cream, it will separate when overheated, so never allow it to simmer or boil.

PARMESAN CHEESE

A classic grating cheese with a deep cheese taste. A little bit of Parmesan goes a very long way. One tablespoon of this medium-fat cheese adds approximately 25 Calories (1.8 g fat) to a recipe. If possible, buy real Italian *Parmaggiano reggiano* and grate it yourself as follows:

Cut the cheese into smallish chunks. Put them in the liquidizer. Blend until finely grated. Store in the refrigerator or the freezer. *Save the rind*: Parmesan rind is one of the magic ingredients of Slim Cuisine. Use a piece of it when simmering certain sauces, soups and ragouts. When the dish is finished, discard the rind. It will have imparted a good Parmesan flavour but very little in the way of Calories and fat.

'And in the evening . . . : I did dig another [pit in the garden] and put our wine in it and my parmazan cheese . . . and some other things.'

Samuel Pepys, *On the Great Fire of London*, 1666

MOZZARELLA CHEESE

72 Calories per oz
4.5 g fat

Another Italian classic. This one melts into a bland, gooey, creamy, pully mass – quite wonderful. Buy real Italian Mozzarella; it is medium fat, and comes packed in liquid.

Other medium-fat cheeses to be used in small quantities
Jarlsberg – A Swiss-type cheese from Denmark
Bruder Basil – A delicately smoked cheese
Feta cheese – A creamy, Greek, ewe's milk cheese. Read the label to be sure you are not buying a full fat Feta. It's very salty; rinse it before using it.
Chevre – There are several of these creamy French goat's milk cheeses that are medium fat. Chevres are a personal favourite of mine in cooking. Again read the label and buy medium or low fat only.

SKIMMED MILK

'There's warmth, comfort, cooing, eye contact, bonding, all those good things associated with nurturing and love, which then all get associated with the taste of milk.'

Dr Stephen Locke quoted in *The International Herald Tribune*, 1987

If you think you hate skimmed milk don't despair. Eventually your palate will adjust to the thinner texture, and you will (if you like milk in the first place) find it perfectly acceptable. In fact, those who use skimmed milk regularly find whole milk quite revolting. It coats the tongue, and feels thick and unpleasantly fatty in the mouth. Forget whole milk, semi-skimmed milk and cream, whether it's double, single, half or one of those new ones that has been relieved of butterfat and filled with polyunsaturates (it will still be chock-full of fat Calories). Do check with your doctor, however, before you switch young children from whole to skimmed. You will find skimmed milk quite useful as a cooking ingredient. Keep powdered skimmed milk in the larder for emergencies.

Seasonings

'Wheat and beef, rice and fish are the prose of food, herbs and spices are its poetry.'

Waverly Root, *Herbs and Spices*, 1980

GARLIC

Don't be afraid of garlic. It is an important part of Slim Cuisine, and adds a wonderful depth of flavour and richness to many preparations. You will find that there are no strong garlicky tastes in any of the recipes in this book that involve cooking, even those that use quantities of the bulb. Slim Cuisine cooking techniques involve steaming, poaching, baking, simmering and boiling; no frying or sautéing in oils or fats. It is these latter techniques that bring out garlic's pungent qualities. On the other hand in salads and dressings that call for raw garlic, the taste will be stronger. By all means in these cases leave out the garlic if you wish.

When shopping, choose your garlic carefully. Lift the bulbs and squeeze them. They should be heavy and firm. Never buy heads that have shrivelled or bruised cloves. (Remember, a clove is one section, a bulb or head is the whole thing.) And never buy garlic that is visibly sprouting. If, when peeling and mincing the cloves, you find that each contains a greenish sprout in the centre, split the clove, remove the sprout and discard it. Store garlic bulbs in a cool well-ventilated part of the kitchen. They should not be tightly wrapped – a basket is the ideal receptacle. Never refrigerate them. Do *not* use garlic salt, garlic powder, or other processed garlic products. They will impart a harsh, rancid and unpleasant taste to your cookery.

When crushing garlic, use a mallet, not a garlic press. The press is an infamous utensil that releases all of garlic's strong, indigestible qualities. The mallet is handy for peeling the cloves as well as crushing them. Hit the clove with the mallet, remove the loosened skin, and proceed.

GINGER

Fresh ginger root has become a supermarket staple. Once you try it, you will be delighted with its clean, bracing flavour. Always peel it first with a paring knife or a swivel-bladed peeler, and then grate it or mince it. If you cannot find the fresh root, substitute ground ginger. It won't be the same as fresh, but it will do.

BLACK PEPPER

Use whole peppercorns cracked in a peppermill, as needed, instead of packaged pre-ground pepper. The taste it imparts to your recipes will be flavourful, not merely sharp. White peppercorns are the same berry as the black ones, at a different stage of ripeness. White pepper is the mature berry with the outer husk removed. Black pepper is slightly underripe. If you abhor black specks in your food, keep a mill filled with white peppercorns for light-coloured food.

SALT

Somehow we have become accustomed to quantities of salt in our food. Try cutting down gradually and learn to savour the taste of good fresh ingredients without their usual cloak of saltiness. Salt is invaluable as a flavour enhancer, and a sprinkle here and there brings out natural flavour in a wonderful way. But those who use it by the handful, who sit down and salt their food liberally before they even taste it, are connoisseurs of salt only, not of food. For the sake of your health, and for the sake of good taste, wean yourself from the excess salt habit. 'Salt to taste', specify the instructions in recipes in this book. Try to make it a sprinkle, not an avalanche.

Canned beans (chick peas, kidney beans, barlotti and cannelini beans, etc.) are excellent larder staples, as is canned tuna, but they contain masses of salt. Wash most of it away by emptying the contents of the can into a colander, and then rinsing well under cold water.

'An overturned Salt-Cellar is to be feared only when it is overturned in a good dish.'

Grimod de la Reyniere, *Almanach des Gourmands*, 1804

SOY SAUCE

An excellent Chinese condiment, very useful with mushrooms. Simmer the fungi in a mixture of stock and wine, with a dash of soy sauce and you won't miss the butter or oil. Read the labels, and buy a brand of soy sauce that does *not* contain monosodium glutamate. All soy sauces contain salt, so wield the salt shaker sparingly when you use the sauce.

SUGAR

Like salt, sugar is very much a matter of taste. And, like salt, sugar
is an amazingly good flavour enhancer. It helps bring out natural
flavours and put them into balance. Unfortunately, most people do
not think of sugar as another seasoning. They think of the sweet
stuff as a major ingredient, and consume an enormous amount of it
each day. The goal should not be to experience an overwhelming
sweetness, but to experience sweetness in concert with other
flavours. Learn to orchestrate ingredients, and to use them with
finesse, so that the overall effect is harmonious. Sugar is just one
part of the orchestra; fight the urge to make it a soloist.

CHILLI PEPPERS

Fresh chillies have found their way into the supermarkets, and
welcome they are, to lovers of incendiary cuisine. There are
thousands of kinds of chilli peppers in the world; out of the
profusion only a few find their way here. You will need to experiment with what your local market has to offer, but if you love edible
fire, as I do, you will find such experimentation pure pleasure.
Fresh chillies can be searingly hot; exercise caution when working
with them. Always wash and trim them under cold, running
water. If your skin is sensitive, or if you have a cut on your hand,
wear rubber gloves. If you don't use gloves, wash your hands *very*
well with soap and water before rubbing your eyes, cuddling your
sweetie or hugging the baby. Two kinds of canned chillies are
convenient to have in the larder. Green chillies (fairly mild) and
jalapeños (very hot). Look for them on the supermarket or
delicatessen shelf that houses Mexican-style foods.

In any recipe in this book containing chilli peppers, reduce or
omit them if you don't like piquant food.

TOMATOES

At certain times of the year there are no tomatoes in the shops, only
a bewildering array of pulpy, pale-pink, tennis-ball-like impostors.
Tomato lovers treat these objects with the scorn they deserve, and
depend upon canned Italian tomatoes until summer comes along,
bringing its ripe bursting-with-flavour, ruby beauties. In the winter, if you long for fresh tomatoes, search for tomatoes from the
Canary Islands and store them at room temperature, in a closed
paper bag. In a few days to a week they will have ripened and may
even taste vaguely like tomatoes, although not like fully-fledged

summer beauties. To peel a fresh tomato, immerse it in boiling water for 10 seconds, then cut out the stem and slip off the skins. The seeds may be removed with your finger. Tomato skins and seeds pass right through the human digestive system untouched, so you won't be losing valuable nutrients. If canned tomatoes seem particularly acidic, add a pinch of sugar when you cook them.

SUN-DRIED TOMATOES

Jars of sun-dried tomatoes, imported from Italy, lurk on the shelves of elegant delicatessens. They are expensive, but – if you are in the mood to indulge yourself – worth splurging on occasionally. The leathery, wrinkled dried tomatoes have a very intense, almost supernatural tomato taste. My favourite of the Italian imports is sun-dried tomato paste. Most sun-dried tomato products are packed in olive oil, therefore you must rid them of oil before using them. Put the amount of tomatoes or paste you wish to use in a small jar, pour in a bit of dry red wine, cover, and shake. Put into a small sieve, and rinse under cold water. This eliminates the oil. Then use them in a sauce, stew or dressing. Because of the intense flavour only a tiny amount is needed at a time, so a jar lasts a long while.

HERBS

'You are trying to find out not what this or that herb is in itself but what it is to you. If something reminds you of new-mown grass – or a paint factory on an off day, Nana's pantry, Uncle Joe's tobacco pouch, the first restaurant where you met your last love, or the last restaurant in which you saw your first – then that is what it is.'

Robert Farrar Capon, *Food for Thought*, 1978

I am delighted to see fresh herbs available in many supermarkets throughout the country. They bring a dimension of freshness and clear flavour that is never realized with the dried variety. A good rule of thumb: use three times the amount of fresh herbs as dried. Do taste as you go, though, and be flexible. Too much of a dried herb will give unpleasant results. And watch the quality of your dried herbs. They become old and musty all too easily. Buy them in small amounts, and store them, tightly covered, in a cool, dark place. To release the flavour components in dried herbs, crumble them between your fingers as you scatter them into the pot.

45

SPICES

Spices are a collection of aromatic barks, seeds, roots and buds that are used to season foods. Buy them in small quantities, store them, tightly covered, in a cool, dark spot, and try not to keep them beyond 6 months. When their oils turn rancid, they are unusable. Through kitchen experiment, learn the tastes of various spices, and learn the way they harmonize or clash with other spices and with various foodstuffs. Soon you will be seasoning food to please your own palate.

WINE

Dry red and white wine, dry sherry and dry vermouth are important Slim Cuisine ingredients. Don't worry about the alcohol (and the alcohol Calories) in such wines. As they cook in your sauces, soups and sautés, the alcohol evaporates away. You are left with an intense and delicious flavour but it won't make anyone drunk, and it won't cause anyone to consume empty alcohol Calories. There is no need to invest in vintage wines for your cookery, but don't use a wine you wouldn't drink on its own. What is bad in the glass is worse in the pot.

WINE VINEGARS

Here is another area for splurging, or try dropping hints here and there, before Christmas or your birthday. 'Designer' vinegars – those elegant ones such as balsamic, sherry, raspberry, etc. – are expensive but they add an exciting dimension to food, especially to fat-free salad dressings and sauces. As with sun-dried tomato paste, a small amount is used at a time so a bottle of interesting vinegar lasts a while.

Equipment

'Except for a few ancient, lethally sharp carbon steel knives, my mother's kitchenware made a mockery of all recipes calling for well insulated pots and enamelled exteriors. As they grew older (they) became so dented on the bottom that they could not stand upright when empty.'

Mimi Sheraton, *From My Mother's Kitchen*, 1972

Non-Reactive Cookware

Cast iron, tin and aluminium cookware will react with acid ingredients such as tomatoes, wine and spinach to produce off flavours and discolorations. To avoid these problems, use *non-reactive* cookware, such as *enamelled* cast iron, stainless steel, flame-proof glass and ceramic, and non-stick coatings such as Tefal and Silverstone. Because no added fat is used in Slim Cuisine, you will find the non-stick cookware invaluable. When choosing such equipment, go for weight. Hefty, heavy-bottomed pots and pans cook evenly and will ensure success. Read the directions that come with your cookware. Many non-stick pots and pans must be seasoned, sometimes by rubbing the non-stick finish with oil (this is the only time you will be using oil in your kitchen), sometimes by simmering milk in the pan.

An enamelled cast-iron frying pan is handy for sautéing – for those times when you want a non-reactive pot, but not a non-stick one (see Sautéed Onions, page 22). If you plan to do a lot of stir-frying (easy to do without fat – see page 159), you might want to invest in a wok. Big ones with cover, steamer rack and non-stick interior are available in cookware departments throughout the country. They work with both gas and electric cookers.

A steamer is an absolute necessity for vegetables. It can be used for fish, chicken breasts and rice as well. Buy a folding one that fits into a large saucepan or, better still, a stock pot with a perforated steamer-basket which fits inside. If necessary, improvise a steamer with a colander set in a saucepan. If you live near a Chinese food shop, consider acquiring a Chinese bamboo steamer that fits in a wok. Such a steamer is fairly inexpensive, easy and versatile to use, and wonderful looking.

For straining, puréeing and draining yoghurt and fromage blanc, have several non-reactive sieves or strainers on hand. Nylon mesh sieves are perfect. Cheesecloth or butter muslin is essential to line the sieve when you use it to make cream cheese (see page 27). If you want to make fat-free icecreams, purées, dips and so on, both a food processor and a liquidizer are invaluable tools. You will use them again and again. A microwave oven, of course, makes a busy cook's life so much easier. And don't forget a fat bouquet of wooden spoons and wire whisks standing in a jar by your work area, and a faithful set of measuring utensils, both spoons and jugs.

RECIPES

'Food imaginatively and lovingly prepared, and eaten
in good company, warms the being with something
more than mere intake of Calories.'

Marjorie Kinnan Rawlings, *Cross Creek Cookery*, 1942

These recipes are meant to guide you through the new techniques of Slim Cuisine. After a while, I hope you will be making up your own, based on the precepts set forth here. When following any recipe make your kitchen life easier by doing the following:

1   First read the recipe through completely.
2   Then have all the ingredients chopped, sliced, diced, poured, measured, etc. Set the prepared ingredients out on your work surface along with any equipment needed. Only then should you begin the actual cooking.

Recipe Notes

1   All ingredients are given in imperial and in metric measurements. Use one or the other, but do not mix measurements in any one recipe.
2   All recipes have approximate Calorie and fat levels per serving. Your idea of a serving may be quite different from mine; everyone has his or her own idea of a proper serving of particular food. To recalculate, multiply the Calories per serving by the number of servings. This will give you the Calories for the entire recipe. Then divide this number by the number of servings you deem appropriate.

Note: see page 214 for advice on planning Slim Cuisine menus for every occasion.

Starters

'Alice tempers her rigidity on the
meals-per-day issue by having a broad view of
what constitutes an hors d'oeuvre.'

Calvin Trillin – *Alice, Let's Eat*, 1978

S tarters should tease the palate, amuse the eyes, and launch the diner into the adventure of a meal. Serve a nibble or two with sherry or sparkling water in the lounge, or serve a beautifully arranged first course at the dining table, but don't overwhelm the diner with an embarrassment of riches or the rest of the meal will be an anticlimax. Many of these starters would work well on a buffet table.

STUFFED POACHED MUSHROOMS

4 Calories per medium (unstuffed) poached mushroom cap
0.1 g fat

This is an absolutely beautiful way to begin a meal or to augment a buffet table. Choose mushrooms large enough to hold a filling but small enough to be picked up easily and popped into the mouth.

Firm, white, medium-sized or button mushrooms	Approx. 3 fl oz/90 ml dry white vermouth
Approx. 3 fl oz/90 ml vegetable stock	Dash or two soy sauce
	Fillings (see suggestions below)

1   Carefully remove the stems from the mushroom caps. Save the stems for another use (Duxelles Cream for instance, see page 170, or Sautéed Mushrooms, see page 26). With a teaspoon, gently even out the mushroom cap opening so it will hold a filling nicely.
2   Pour the stock, vermouth and soy sauce into a non-stick frying pan that will hold the mushroom caps in one layer. Bring the liquid to a boil. Add the mushroom caps in one layer, stem side up, reduce heat, cover the pan and simmer for 2–3 minutes. Uncover, raise heat and cook, tossing the mushrooms in the pan for a minute or so, until the caps are cooked but still quite firm, and the liquid is reduced and syrupy. Remove from the pan and drain upside down on paper towels.
3   With a teaspoon, neatly fill each cap with a filling of your choice. Use several different fillings of contrasting colours and textures for dramatic effect. Arrange on a serving platter. These may be prepared an hour ahead of time if desired.

Fillings:
The best, from both a visual and a taste point of view, are Beetroot Purée, 4 Calories per tablespoon, 0 g fat (see page 164), and Mint Raita, 2.8 Calories per tablespoon, 0.03 g fat (see page 184). But try these also (with Calorie and fat values given per teaspoon):

Pesto	(page 145)	9.1 Calories 0.4 g fat
Tzatziki	(page 57)	5.0 Calories 0.03 g fat
Tonnato	(page 58)	8.3 Calories 0.03 g fat
Liptauer Cheese	(page 54)	5.6 Calories 0.03 g fat
Creamy Herb Dressing	(page 183)	3.3 Calories 0.03 g fat
Duxelles Cream	(page 170)	2.3 Calories 0.03 g fat
Mustard Cream	(page 170)	4.3 Calories 0.03 g fat

MUSHROOM RAVIOLI

Makes 50 ravioli
13 Calories per piece
0.1 g fat

Won Ton wrappers (squares of noodle dough) are available in Chinese groceries. These delicate, mushroom-stuffed triangles are very special. Do not overwhelm them with sauce or the intense mushroom taste will not come through.

---

2 packages Won Ton wrappers *(about 50 wrappers)*	*1 pt/600 ml Duxelles (see page 168)* *Fresh, washed spinach leaves*

---

1 Sprinkle your work surface with flour. Have 2 clean teatowels at hand. Have a small bowl filled with water on your work surface.
2 Put 1 Won Ton wrapper flat on the work surface (keep the remainder covered with a clean teatowel). Place a teaspoon of Duxelles in the centre of the wrapper. Dip your finger in the water and moisten the edge of the wrapper all around. Fold over to form a triangle and press the edges together so they adhere. Put the wrapper on the floured surface and cover with the second clean teatowel. Repeat until all the wrappers and Duxelles are used up. (The ravioli may be frozen at this point. Dust two baking sheets with flour. Place the ravioli on the sheets in one layer, cover with cling film and freeze. When they are frozen solid, put them in a plastic bag and store in the freezer until needed. Do not thaw before cooking.)

3   Bring water to the boil in the bottom of the steamer. Line the steamer basket with spinach or lettuce leaves. Place the ravioli in one layer, on the greens. You will need to do this in several batches. Steam, covered, for 6–8 minutes, until tender. If they were frozen, steam for 10–12 minutes. Serve with Smooth Tomato Sauce (see page 151), or with Hungarian Green Sauce (see page 144). Ladle a bit of sauce over each serving, but do not swamp them.

4   Alternatively, do as my housekeeper Mary Hardy suggests; serve these mushroom-filled morsels as dumplings on beef stew. (See pages 103–4 for beef stew recipes).

LIPTAUER CHEESE

12 Calories per tablespoon
0.1 g fat
(traditional Liptauer cheese: 48 Calories per tablespoon)

Conventionally, this Hungarian cheese spread is made with full fat cheese and soured cream. My version has approximately ½ the Calories of the original, yet there is virtually no difference in taste. Will fill five coeur à la creme moulds.

---

1 carton (1 lb 1½ oz) skimmed milk quark	Salt and freshly ground pepper to taste
3 fl oz/90 ml buttermilk	2 teaspoons caraway seeds
1 tablespoon sweet Hungarian paprika	Several dashes of tabasco sauce
	1 teaspoon chopped capers

---

1   Combine all ingredients in a bowl. Beat to a smooth paste.
2   This may be served in coeur à la creme moulds (perforated heart-shaped moulds). Line the moulds with damp cheese-cloth leaving an overhang. Scrape an equal portion of the mixture into each mould. Fold up the overhang to cover. Place the moulds, perforated side down, on a rack placed on a baking sheet. Refrigerate overnight to drain. Unmould, arrange attractively on a bed of greens and serve.
3   If you do not have any coeur à la creme moulds, scrape the mixture into a colander lined with damp cheesecloth, and let drain overnight. Serve with thin-sliced wholemeal bread or with slices of cucumber and courgette. Spread the mixture on the bread or vegetable slices.

Another serving suggestion: Mound the mixture into halved seeded and ribbed red, yellow, green or purple peppers. Serve with crudités for dipping. (Crudités are raw vegetables, cut into bite-sized pieces. Try cauliflower, broccoli, courgette, cucumber, carrot, turnip, radishes etc.)

Vary this recipe with different ingredients. Try roasted garlic purée and chopped chives; finely chopped mushrooms simmered in stock until tender and dry, seasoned with a touch of nutmeg and cayenne pepper; puréed roasted red pepper with a squeeze of lemon juice . . . The possibilities are endless!

SMOKED FISH PATÉ

Makes ½ pt/300 ml
30 Calories per tablespoon
0.9 g fat
(traditional Smoked Fish Mousse: 60 Calories per tablespoon, 5.9 g fat)

Twin Marks, a loyal fan of Slim Cuisine, made this for a buffet, and the murmur went round, 'Have you tasted the fish paté? It's fabulous!' This is a great people-pleaser.

6–8 oz/240 g smoked trout or mackerel fillets, flaked
⅖ pt/240 ml yoghurt cream cheese or fromage blanc cream cheese (see page 27)

2 tablespoons chopped fresh chives

---

1 Combine all ingredients in the bowl of a food processor.
2 Process until very smooth. Scrape into a crock and refrigerate overnight for the flavours to blend.
3 Serve with thin slices of wholemeal bread, toasted or not, as you prefer.

DILLED SMOKED SALMON SALAD

Makes ¾ pt/450 ml
26 Calories per tablespoon
1 g fat

This tastes exactly as if it were made with creme fraiche. If you wish, pack it into a fish-shaped mould and refrigerate it overnight. The next day, unmould it onto a sea of greens.

2 tablespoons drained yoghurt	4 tablespoons chopped fresh dill
2 tablespoons buttermilk	½ lb/225 g smoked salmon,
⅓ pt/198 ml skimmed milk quark	shredded
4 oz/112 g chopped fresh parsley	Freshly ground pepper to taste

1   Combine all ingredients. Mix gently with a wooden spoon.
2   Scrape the mixture into a crock. Refrigerate overnight for flavours to blend.
3   Serve with chicory leaves and radicchio leaves. Each diner spoons a bit of the mixture into a leaf.

KATHLEEN EDWARDS'S TUNA MOUSSE

Serves 8
43 Calories per serving
0.2 g fat

This creamy mousse is attractive in a fish-shaped mould. Decorate it beautifully for a buffet table.

3 teaspoons gelatine	Salt and freshly ground pepper to
2 tablespoons white wine vinegar	taste
½ pt/300 ml boiling chicken or	8 oz/240 g tuna in brine, very well
vegetable stock	drained
½ small onion, finely chopped	4 tablespoons fromage blanc
1 clove garlic	Garnish (cucumber, parsley,
¼ teaspoon dried tarragon	watercress, fresh tarragon, etc.
	as desired)

1   Place gelatine and vinegar in the liquidizer container and let stand for one minute.
2   Add the chicken or vegetable stock and blend.
3   Add all remaining ingredients except fromage blanc and garnish. Blend until perfectly smooth, about 1 minute.
4   Pour the tuna mixture into a bowl and let sit at room temperature until thickened but not set.
5   Stir the fromage blanc into the tuna mixture. Pour into a mould and refrigerate until set.
6   To serve, unmould onto a serving plate and decorate with fresh herbs, watercress, etc. Serve with Melba toast or motzah crackers if you wish.

TZATZIKI

Makes ⅘ pt/480 ml as a dip, 1⅕ pt/720 ml as a sauce
15 Calories per tablespoon
0.1 g fat
(traditional Tzatziki: 30 Calories per tablespoon, 2 g fat)

Serve this zesty Greek mixture as a dip with toasted pitta bread triangles, or as a sauce for steamed or grilled fish or grilled lean meat (Goose Skirt Steak, page 106, for instance.) The meat juices mingling with the cold Tzatziki are absolutely delicious.

1⅗ pt/960 ml skimmed milk yoghurt	2 large cloves garlic, minced
2 large cucumbers	1½ teaspoons white wine vinegar
Salt	Freshly ground pepper to taste

1   Drain the yoghurt for 24 hours (as described in the yoghurt cheese recipe) if you want to serve the Tzatziki as a dip. To serve it as a sauce, drain it for 6–7 hours only.
2   Peel the cucumbers. Cut them in half lengthwise. Use a teaspoon to scrape out the seeds. Discard them. Grate the cucumbers into a colander. Salt them and allow to drain for ½ hour. This draws out their bitterness.
3   Place the minced garlic and vinegar in a small bowl and allow to marinate while the cucumbers are draining.
4   Rinse the drained cucumbers, squeeze them as dry as possible and blot them on paper towels. Place in the bowl with the marinated garlic. Add the drained yoghurt and a few grindings of fresh pepper and stir. Serve at once or store in the refrigerator. It will keep for several days, and improve in flavour each day.

TURKEY AND MELON WITH MINT PESTO

45 Calories per serving
1.2 g fat

This is a colourful starter and the combination of tastes and textures is unusual and pleasing. The plates may be arranged an hour or so before serving. The Pesto may be made days in advance.

Ripe melon	Slim Cuisine Pesto made with fresh
Thinly sliced smoked turkey breast	mint leaves (see page 145)
(available in delicatessens)	Fresh mint leaves

1   Slice melon thinly. Cut off rind. Wrap each slice in a slice of turkey breast.
2   Arrange 3 wrapped slices on each plate. Place a blob of Pesto on the base of the plate. Garnish with fresh mint leaves and serve.

TONNATO SAUCE

Makes ¾ pt/450 ml
25 Calories per tablespoon
0.1 g fat
(traditional tonnato sauce: 73 Calories per tablespoon, 2.6 g fat)

Tonnato is an Italian tuna mayonnaise and one of my favourite cold sauces. It is traditionally served on slices of roasted veal or turkey breast. It is good as a first course with lightly steamed, chilled vegetables. It is also heavenly spread on toast.

½ pt/300 ml yoghurt cheese or fromage blanc (see page 27)	*Juice of ½ lemon*
Purée from 1 head baked garlic (see page 29)	*2 teaspoons capers*
2 tins (7 oz/196 g each) of tuna packed in brine, very well drained	*Salt and freshly ground pepper to taste*

1   Combine all the ingredients in the container of a food processor, and process until very smooth. Scrape into a crock or bowl and refrigerate for at least a day. (The sauce will keep for a week and improve in flavour each day.)
2   Serve as a sauce or dip with crudités or lightly steamed vegetables.

REMOULADE SAUCE

Makes approx. 2 pt/1,200 ml sauce
12 Calories per tablespoon
0.1 g fat

This sauce is versatile as a dip, a sandwich spread or a sauce for julienned celeriac, cold poached chicken, steamed prawns or very lean, rare cold beef.

2 pt/1,200 ml Slim Cuisine
  'mayonnaise' made from
  yoghurt or fromage blanc or a
  mixture of both (see page 27)
2 teaspoons Dijon mustard
4 tablespoons capers, rinsed
4 tablespoons chopped cornichons
  (small, sour gherkins)

4 tablespoons chopped fresh parsley
1 teaspoon paprika
6 spring onions, chopped, green
  and white parts
Few drops tabasco sauce
½ tablespoon dried tarragon,
  crumbled

Mix all the ingredients together with a wire whisk. Allow to ripen
in the refrigerator for at least 1 hour before using.

HUMMUS

Makes 1 pt/600 ml
23 Calories per tablespoon
0.4 g fat
(traditional hummus: 48 Calories per tablespoon, 1.4 g fat)

A low-fat version of a classic Middle Eastern chick pea spread. The
texture is rich and unctuous.

1½ tablespoons sesame seeds
2 tins (15½ oz/434 g each) of chick
  peas, drained (reserve ¼ to ⅓ of
  the liquid from one tin)

Purée from 1 head roasted garlic or
  2–3 large raw garlic cloves
Juice of 2 large lemons

1   Toast the sesame seeds in a small heavy frying pan. Stir them
    constantly and do not allow them to scorch.
2   Place the sesame seeds in a liquidizer and process until they
    are pulverized.
3   Add all the remaining ingredients including ¼ of one tin of the
    chick pea liquid. Process until very smooth and creamy; the
    consistency of mashed potatoes. Add a little more of the chick
    pea liquid if the mixture is too thick and add a bit more lemon
    juice if you prefer a sharper taste. Serve as a sandwich spread,
    or a dip with toasted pitta bread wedges and raw vegetables.

Variations:
1 Mix hummus with an equal amount of quark and use as a filling
  for baked potatoes or potato cases (see page 172).
2 Thin with chicken or vegetable stock to a sauce-like consistency,
  and toss with hot pasta.

ALOO CHAT

Serves 4
160 Calories per serving
0.2 g fat

Potatoes, coriander and chilli make up my favourite Indian starter. It is sour, spicy and stimulating.

---

2 small, fresh green chillies, stemmed, seeded and minced
8 medium new potatoes, steamed until tender and diced
4 tablespoons coarsely chopped fresh coriander

4 tablespoons thinly sliced spring onions
Salt to taste
4 tablespoons lemon juice

Gently toss all ingredients together. Allow to sit at room temperature for at least ½ hour before serving.

SHASHI'S PARMA ALOO (STUFFED POTATOES, INDIAN STYLE)

Makes 8 pieces
51 Calories per piece
0.1 g fat

This glorious dish is an old family recipe of Shashi Rattan's. I have omitted the oil and substituted lemon juice for hard-to-find mango powder. As the potatoes bake, the spicy coating blackens in places and forms a delicious crust. Parma Aloo are good served hot or cold. I think they taste best eaten with the fingers.

½ teaspoon ground turmeric
½ teaspoon garam masala
¼ teaspoon ground cumin

Juice of ½ small lemon
1 tablespoon tomato paste
8 small new potatoes

---

1   Preheat oven to 350° F (180° C/Gas Mark 4).
2   Combine everything except potatoes in a bowl. Mix to a paste.
3   Peel potatoes. Pierce in several places with skewer or a fork. Cut a lengthwise wedge (½ in/1.27 cm wide) out of each potato. Rub the hole with spice paste and insert the wedge back in. Rub the potatoes all over with the remaining paste.
4   Place a rack on a baking tray and arrange the potatoes on the rack. Bake for 30–40 minutes, turning every 10 minutes, until tender. Serve at once.

Soup

'Beautiful soup, so rich and green
Waiting in a hot tureen.'

Lewis Carroll, *Alice's Adventures in Wonderland*, 1865

A steam-wreathed tureen of soup, emitting delectable and tantalizing whiffs of comfort, never fails to delight even the grumpiest diner. Soup nourishes the soul as well as the body. It evokes memories of cosy evenings by the hearth, while the cruel winter elements rage outside. Soup slides down soothingly – smooth and easy – making the diner feel loved and indulged. I am happy to tell you that Slim Cuisine soups are nutrient-dense but not Calorie-dense; you can wallow in that lovely, cosseted feeling without wallowing in fat as well. Several Slim Cuisine techniques make this splendid state of affairs possible; use them to reduce the fat and Calorie levels of any soup recipe you might come across:

1   Never use oil, butter or margarine to sauté the vegetables that form the flavour base of a soup. Use the stock-sauté method, or the onion infusion.

2   The classic way of enriching many soups is with butter, egg yolk and cream. Don't do it! The best way to enrich a creamy vegetable purée soup is with the vegetable itself. Use more of the vegetable than called for in a traditional recipe. When cooked, purée the soup in a liquidizer or processor, or put it through a food mill. It will be rich and creamy. In some cases, you might want to purée half of the soup, then combine the puréed and unpuréed portions. This makes a lovely, interesting texture.

3   Substitute low-fat fromage blanc, yoghurt, quark or skimmed milk, for sour cream, creme fraiche or cream.

4   Use potato for body and thickening. It adds plenty of nutrients but few Calories and no fat.

5   Baked vegetables, especially baked garlic, give wonderful depth to low-fat soups. One of the soups in this section is made up entirely of baked vegetables. It is satisfying enough to be a main dish, yet it has only 98 Calories per 8 fl oz/240 ml serving! Experiment with adding various puréed baked vegetables to soup for flavour and body.

6   Splash wine and spirits generously into your soups. In the simmering, the alcohol (and alcohol Calories) evaporate but the flavour remains. For instance, red wine and cognac combine to add richness to French Onion Soup (see page 69). Without them, this extremely low-fat soup would have a somewhat anaemic taste.

Soup Savvy

Do you love to begin a meal with a nice hearty bowlful of steaming soup? If you do, you will be pleased to know that soup has been shown to be a splendid diet food. Recent research studies at several American universities have suggested that soup, eaten in large quantities before a meal, results in fewer total Calories ingested in that meal. In fact the more soup, the fewer total Calories. Furthermore, the study suggests that enthusiastic soup eaters who eat the hot, soothing stuff regularly, are much more likely to keep to their target weight over the long term than non-soup eaters.

The liquidizer is used to purée many soups. Never fill the liquidizer jar with hot soup. When the machine is switched on, the hot liquid will surge up, blow off the cover, splash and burn the cook, and make a spectacular mess on the ceiling. Let the soup cool somewhat first, then fill the jar less than halfway.

HERBED TOMATO SOUP

Makes 3⅕ pt/1920 ml
15 Calories per 10 fl oz/300 ml
0.0 g fat

This soup, adapted from Barbara Kafka's *Food for Friends,* is so easy that it is almost embarrassing. 'How did you make this?' your friends will exclaim as they savour every sip. Remain smugly silent. Fresh herbs are on sale all year round in many supermarkets. As for the tomato liquid, it is almost *free!* When using tinned tomatoes *never* throw the precious liquid away. Save it for ambrosial concoctions like this. If the juice is too acidic for your taste, add a pinch of sugar. (Step 1 may be done in advance. Complete Step 2 just before serving.) And note the method of measuring the herbs in a graduated measuring jug. It's easy and exact.

2⅕ pts/1,320 ml chicken or vegetable stock	⅕ pt/120 ml fresh parsley, finely chopped
2⅕ pts/1,320 ml tomato liquid (drained from tinned Italian tomatoes)	Pinch sugar (optional)
	3 cloves garlic, crushed or minced
⅕ pt/120 ml fresh basil, finely shredded	Salt and freshly ground pepper to taste
⅕ pt/120 ml fresh dill, snipped	½ teaspoon tabasco sauce
	Pinch cayenne pepper
	Juice of 1 lemon

1   Combine the stock, tomato liquid and herbs in a non-reactive pot. Simmer for 15 minutes.
2   Stir in remaining ingredients. Serve at once.

RED CABBAGE SOUP

Makes 2½ pt/1,500 ml
81 Calories per 10 fl oz/300 ml
0.6 g fat

A dazzlingly purple soup with a homely, comforting taste. Perfect cold-weather fare.

¼ pt/150 ml chopped shallots
3 pts/1,800 ml chicken stock
1 medium baking potato, peeled and coarsely chopped
1 medium red cabbage, cored and shredded

1 large tart apple, peeled, cored and coarsely chopped
Salt and freshly ground pepper to taste
Freshly ground nutmeg
4–6 tablespoons low fat yoghurt at room temperature

---

1   Combine shallots and 4 fl oz/120 ml of the stock in a non-reactive soup pot. Cover and bring to a boil.
2   Uncover. Reduce heat slightly and simmer briskly until the liquid has evaporated and the shallots are beginning to stick to the pan.
3   Toss in the potatoes and an additional splash of stock. Toss, stirring and scraping up the browned bits on the bottom of the pot.
4   When the potatoes begin to brown slightly, toss in the cabbage and the apple. Toss and cook over medium heat for 2–3 minutes.
5   Pour in the remaining stock. Season to taste. Bring to a boil, reduce heat and simmer, partially covered, for 15 minutes, until the cabbage and potatoes are tender but not mushy. Season to taste and cool slightly.
6   In a liquidizer, purée the soup. Do this in several batches. (The

Fish and chips (page 83 and page 175)
the Slim Cuisine way is a revelation. One tastes the
natural flavours of the food, not a surfeit of grease.
Trout with fresh herbs and lemon zest, steamed until
succulent in greaseproof paper (page 80).

soup may be made in advance to this point and refrigerated for a day or two.)

7   At serving time, heat the soup until it is piping hot. Serve it in clear glass bowls, to show off its gorgeous purple colour. Swirl one tablespoon of yoghurt decoratively over the surface of each serving, and sprinkle on some freshly grated nutmeg.

TURNIP SOUP

Makes 3⅕ pt/1,920 ml
61 Calories per 10 fl oz/300 ml
0.4 g fat

The garlic may seem excessive, but (if the garlic is fresh) there is *no* vulgar garlicky taste in this soup, just a gentle, nutty sweetness. Although there is no cream, only a few ounces of skimmed milk, the texture is velvety and creamy. Those who overdosed on turnips at boarding school may want to skip this one, but I feel that the humble root reaches exquisite heights in this soup. This also works well with parsnips, swedes or a combination of root vegetables.

3⅕ pts/1,920 ml peeled,
   coarsely-diced small white
   turnips
15 large cloves garlic, peeled
1⅗ pts/960 ml stock

1 orange
4 fl oz/120 ml skimmed milk
Salt and freshly ground pepper to
   taste

---

1   Combine turnips, garlic and stock in a non-reactive soup pot. Bring to a boil. Skim off scum.
2   Reduce heat and simmer partially covered until the turnips and garlic are tender, 15–20 minutes. Cool slightly.
3   Purée the soup in a liquidizer and return to the pot. The texture should be very smooth and velvety.
4   With a citrus zester, zest the orange rind right over the pot so that the rind goes in and orange oil as well. Save the orange for another use (a private nibble, perhaps). Stir in the milk and seasonings to taste. Reheat gently, stirring occasionally. Serve piping hot. (This soup may be made in advance and refrigerated for several days.)

Mixed soft fruits and fresh mint complement
the creamy textures of pan-sautéed chicken breasts and
yoghurt-honey dressing (page 115).

Variation:

Omit the orange rind. Prepare red pepper purée from baked or grilled red peppers (see page 31). Swirl a blob of red pepper purée decoratively onto the surface of each serving of soup.

RED PEPPER SOUP

Makes 3½ pts/2,100 ml
61 Calories per 10 fl oz/300 ml
0.3 g fat

Red peppers are fleshy, sweet and brilliantly coloured. They give all three properties to this gentle soup. Potatoes add additional substance and fromage blanc gives a touch of creaminess with no added fat.

2 medium onions, chopped
2⅖ pts/1,440 ml stock
2 fl oz/60 ml dry white wine
1 medium baking potato, peeled and coarsely diced
Salt and freshly ground pepper to taste

8 large red peppers, trimmed, ribbed and coarsely diced
1 teaspoon dried thyme, crumbled
Cayenne pepper to taste
Non-fat fromage blanc or fromage frais

1   Combine onions and 4 fl oz/120 ml of the stock in a soup pot. Cover and bring to a boil. Reduce heat and allow to steam for 5 minutes.
2   Uncover and continue cooking for another few minutes until the mixture begins to brown and stick to the bottom of the pan. Splash in the wine, and boil, scraping the browned bits off the bottom of the pot.
3   Stir in the potato and 4 more fl oz/120 ml of stock. Cover and cook over medium heat for 5 minutes. Uncover and stir once or twice during this time. After 5 minutes, splash in a bit more stock and again scrape any browned bits from the bottom of the pot. Season the mixture with a bit of salt and a generous grinding of pepper.
4   Toss in the peppers, the thyme and a bit of cayenne. Pour in the remaining stock and simmer, partially covered, until the vegetables are tender, about ½ hour. Cool.
5   In batches, purée the soup in a liquidizer. Pour it through a fine sieve into the soup pot. Rub the solids through with a wooden spoon or a rubber spatula. The tough pepper skins will be left behind in the sieve. Discard them. (The soup may be cooled at this point, and refrigerated for a few days.)

6   Gently heat the soup. Add more salt, black pepper and cayenne pepper to taste. Crumble in a touch more dried thyme if you feel that it is needed.
7   Serve with a dollop of fromage frais on each serving.

BEAN SOUP

Makes 3½ pts/2,100 ml
162 Calories per 10 fl oz/300 ml
2 g fat

This is a magnificent and sophisticated soup, full of intriguing textures and tastes floating around in perfect harmony. It has echoes of the culinary traditions of both Mexico and Thailand. Jalapeños are fiery Mexican peppers. Look for small tins of jalapeños in vinegar in delicatessens and some supermarkets. They are to be found where other Mexican foods (chilli, tortilla chips etc.) are found. The use of tinned beans makes the preparation of this soup quick and easy. Always rinse tinned beans before use so that a good proportion of their added salt is washed away.

---

1 tin (1 lb 12 oz/784 g) Italian tomatoes
1 small tin (4 oz/112 g) sliced jalapeños in vinegar
1⅘ pt/1,080 ml stock
3 tins (1 lb/453 g each) barlotti beans, drained and rinsed
1 rounded tablespoon tomato paste
½ teaspoon dried oregano, crumbled
A few grinds of black pepper

¼ pt/150 ml fresh parsley, coarsely chopped
Several sprigs fresh coriander, coarsely chopped
1 bunch spring onions, trimmed and sliced thin
1 large clove garlic, minced
4 tablespoons red wine vinegar
6 tablespoons water
Juice of 1 lime
6 tablespoons Parmesan cheese

---

1   Pour the tomatoes and their juices into a liquidizer. Add approximately ¼ of the jalapeños and ¼ of the jalapeño juice (use less if you want a tame soup, more if you pride yourself on your asbestos palate). Purée. Put the purée through a non-reactive sieve so that the seeds are left behind.
2   Pour the sieved mixture into a non-reactive soup pot. Add the stock, beans, tomato paste, oregano and pepper. Simmer, uncovered for 20 minutes. Roughly mash some of the beans in the pot with a potato masher. (The recipe may be made in advance to this point. Cool and refrigerate until needed.)
3   Meanwhile, combine chopped parsley, chopped coriander,

spring onions, garlic, vinegar and water in a small saucepan or frying pan. Boil, stirring occasionally until almost dry. Stir this mixture into the simmering bean soup.

4   Stir in the lime juice. Sprinkle on the Parmesan cheese. Stir gently until the cheese melts into the soup. Taste and add more lime juice, pepper or oregano to taste. If you feel it needs it, add a bit of salt, but it probably won't need much.

CARROT SOUP

Makes 3 pts/1,800 ml
89 Calories per 10 fl oz/300 ml
0.4 g fat

This burnt-orange soup has two versions: the first elegant, smooth and piquant; the second chunky, homely and mild.

1½ lb/680 g carrots, peeled and coarsely chopped	*½ teaspoon ground nutmeg*
2 stalks celery, coarsely chopped	*Freshly ground pepper*
5 cloves garlic, peeled	*2 pts/1,200 ml stock*
1 large onion, coarsely chopped	*Salt to taste*
3 fl oz/90 ml stock	*3 tablespoons non-fat fromage blanc, at room temperature*
3 fl oz/90 ml dry sherry	*1 rounded tablespoon Dijon mustard*
1 baking potato, peeled and coarsely diced	*1 tablespoon snipped fresh dill*

1   Combine carrots, celery, garlic, onion, 3 fl oz/90 ml of stock and 2 fl oz/60 ml of sherry in a non-reactive soup pot. Cover and bring to a boil. Allow to boil, uncovering to stir occasionally, until almost dry.

2   Uncover. Let cook for a few moments more until the mixture begins to burn just a bit and to stick to the bottom of the pot. Splash in 1 fl oz/30 ml of sherry and boil, scraping up the brown bits on the bottom of the pan with a wooden spoon.

3   Toss in the potato. Cook over medium heat for a minute or two, stirring. Stir in the nutmeg and pepper and toss to coat the vegetables with the spices.

4   Stir in the stock and salt. Cover and bring to a boil. Reduce heat and simmer, partially covered, until the vegetables are tender, 20–30 minutes. Cool slightly.

5   Put the soup into the liquidizer in batches. Purée to a smooth, velvety consistency. (The soup may be made in advance to this point. Cool and refrigerate until needed.) Return to the soup pot and bring to a simmer.

6   Remove the soup from the heat. Whisk together the fromage
     blanc and the mustard. Gradually stir some of the soup into
     the mustard mixture. Then, slowly, stir the mustard-soup
     mixture into the soup, along with the dill.

Variation:
Instead of puréeing the soup to a velvety smoothness, pulse the
liquidizer on and off a few times, so that the soup is chunky. Omit
the fromage blanc and the mustard. Stir in the dill.

ONION SOUP

Makes 3½ pts/2,100 ml
69 Calories per 10 fl oz/300 ml
0.2 g fat
(traditional onion soup 263 Calories, 13 g fat)

French onion soup without butter or oil? Yes, if you utilize two Slim
Cuisine techniques: browned onions and spring onion/shallot
infusion. A good portion of the long cooking time is untended
simmering, so you need not feel tied to the cooker for the whole
time.

3½ pts/2,100 ml thinly sliced Spanish onions	3 fl oz/120 ml dry red wine
5 leeks, cleaned, trimmed and thinly sliced	1 piece of Parmesan rind
16 fl oz/480 ml stock	4 fl oz/120 ml cognac
6 fl oz/180 ml dry red wine	1 bunch spring onions, trimmed and thinly sliced
1 tablespoon plain white flour	3 shallots, chopped
3⅕ pts/1,920 ml stock, brought to a boil	Salt and pepper to taste

1   Combine onions, leeks and 16 fl oz/480 ml stock in a deep soup
     pot. Cover and bring to a boil. Reduce heat a bit and simmer
     briskly for 10 minutes.
2   Uncover. Simmer for 35–40 minutes, stirring occasionally. At
     this point, the onions will be turning amber brown and dry.
     Stir constantly as they cook a few minutes more. They will
     soon begin to stick and burn. Keep stirring over low heat for
     about 10 minutes more. As you stir, scrape up the browned
     deposits on the bottom of the pot. Turn up the heat a bit.
     Splash in 3 fl oz red wine. Boil until dry, stirring and scraping
     like mad.
3   Turn the heat to low, and stir in the flour. Stir for about 3
     minutes over low heat.

4   Gradually add the hot stock, and 3 fl oz/120 ml red wine, stirring all the while. Add the Parmesan rind. Partially cover the pot and simmer for 40 minutes, skimming and stirring occasionally.
5   During the last 20 minutes, stir the cognac into the soup. Then combine the spring onions, shallots and 3 fl oz/90 ml red wine in a small saucepan or frying pan. Bring to a boil, reduce heat, and simmer briskly until almost all liquid has evaporated. Stir this mixture into the simmering soup.
6   When the soup has simmered for 40 minutes, remove from the heat. Season to taste. Remove the Parmesan rind. Serve piping hot.

SOUP OF BAKED VEGETABLES

Makes 2½ pts/1,500 ml
98 Calories per 10 fl oz/300 ml
0.5 g fat

Do not be daunted by the number of steps in this recipe. It is *very* easy and makes one of the richest most deliciously satisfying soups you have ever eaten. Serve it with crusty bread spread with low-fat quark, and you have a meal.

---

4 small aubergines, about ½ pound/225 g each	32 fl oz/960 ml stock
1 large Spanish onion	Salt and freshly ground pepper to taste
2 heads garlic	½ teaspoon dried thyme, crumbled
2 red peppers	½ teaspoon dried tarragon, crumbled
1 tin (1 lb 12 oz/784 g) Italian tomatoes, well drained	⅛ teaspoon allspice
1 tablespoon tomato paste	2 fl oz/60 ml cognac

---

1   Preheat the oven to 425°F (220°C/Gas Mark 6). Prick the aubergines in several places with a skewer or the prongs of a fork.
2   Spread the aubergines, onion, garlic and red peppers on a large baking sheet. Bake for 1 hour. Turn the peppers once or twice during this time.
3   After 1 hour, remove all vegetables except onion from the oven and allow to cool. The peppers should be quite black. If so, close them up in a paper bag for a few minutes. (If they are not charred all over, place them under the grill first, turning frequently, until they are thoroughly blackened. Then, remove from grill and close up in a paper bag.)

4   Place the drained tomatoes in the liquidizer. Cut the stems from the aubergines and strip off the skins. Place the pulp in the liquidizer. Purée. Push through a fine sieve into a soup pot so that all the tomato and aubergine seeds are left behind. Discard the seeds.
5   Squeeze the garlic cloves so that the softened garlic purée pops from the skins. Add the purée to the pot.
6   Remove the peppers from the bag and strip off the charred skins. Discard the skins and the seeds. Purée the peppers in the liquidizer and add to the pot.
7   By this time, the onion will be soft. Remove it from the oven. (Work with an oven glove; the onion will be hot!) Cut off the stem and root ends and strip off the first two layers. Cut, into quarters, place in the liquidizer and purée. Add to the pot.
8   Stir in the tomato paste, the stock and all the seasoning. Simmer, partially covered, for 30 minutes, stirring occasionally.
9   Stir in the cognac and simmer for 5 minutes more. Serve piping hot. This soup may be prepared two days ahead and refrigerated. The flavour will improve each day.

SPLIT PEA SOUP

Makes 2½ pts/1,500 ml
228 Calories per 10 fl oz/300 ml
2 g fat

The baked garlic is optional in this hearty soup, but I strongly recommend that you try it; it gives a wonderful dimension to the pale green brew. The soup can be made in advance, but it will thicken dramatically in the refrigerator. Thin it with stock before reheating.

½ lb/225 g split peas, rinsed and picked over	Purée from 1–2 heads baked garlic (optional)
2 baking potatoes peeled and cubed	4 tablespoons Parmesan cheese
3⅕ pts/1,920 ml stock	Salt
1 large onion, chopped	

---

1   Combine peas, potatoes and 32 fl oz/960 ml stock in a saucepan. Bring to a boil, reduce heat and simmer briskly, partially covered, until peas and potatoes are tender, about 40 minutes. Cool slightly.
2   While the vegetables are simmering, sauté the onions in stock according to the Slim Cuisine method: combine onions and 4 fl

oz/120 ml stock in a frying pan. Cover and bring to the boil. Uncover and boil for 5 minutes or so until the liquid has almost cooked away. Reduce heat and simmer until the onions are just about dry and beginning to stick and burn. Pour in a splash of stock and boil, stirring and scraping up the browned bits on the bottom of the frying pan.

3   When the peas and potatoes are tender, push them through a fine sieve or put them through a food mill and return them to the pot. Add the sautéed onions and the remaining stock and stir in the garlic purée, if used.

4   Simmer the soup for approximately 15 minutes. Add the cheese and stir gently until it melts into the soup. Taste and add a touch of salt if needed. Serve piping hot.

WILD MUSHROOM SOUP

Makes 2½ pts/1,500 ml
45 Calories per 10 fl oz/300 ml
0.7 g fat

The dried mushrooms are available in delicatessens and speciality food shops. Chinese and Japanese dried mushrooms may be substituted if necessary. The soup may be made a few days in advance. If fresh oyster mushrooms are available, use them as part of the measure of fresh mushrooms. They will impart a lovely, buttery quality to the soup.

---

1 oz/28 g dried Boletus edulis (cepes)	2½ pts/1,500 ml stock
½ oz/14 g dried morels	4 oz/112 g chopped shallots
2 lb/900 g fresh mushrooms, cleaned and quartered	2 cloves garlic, minced
Approx. ½ pt/300 ml medium sherry	1 teaspoon dried tarragon, crumbled
Dash or two of soy sauce	Salt and pepper to taste
	Piece of Parmesan cheese rind

---

1   Rinse dried mushrooms well under cold running water. Put them in a bowl with hot water to cover generously. Let soak for 1 hour.

2   In a heavy, large, non-stick frying pan, combine the fresh mushrooms with the sherry and soy sauce. If your frying pan is too small, do this step in several batches. Simmer briskly until the mixture is almost dry. Stir frequently and do not let them scorch or brown. Scrape the mixture into a large pot.

3   Strain the soaking water from the dried mushrooms through a sieve lined with cheesecloth or a coffee filter to eliminate grit and sand. Rinse the mushrooms well under cold running water. Discard any tough stems and chop the mushrooms coarsely.

4   Add the soaked mushrooms and their filtered water to the fresh mushrooms in the pot.

5   In a small frying pan, combine the shallots, garlic, tarragon, 4 fl oz/120 ml stock and a splash of sherry. Boil until almost dry. Add to the pot.

6   Add the remaining stock, a bit of salt and pepper, and the Parmesan rind. Bring to a boil, reduce heat and simmer, partially covered, for 1 hour. Discard the cheese rind. Taste and add more salt and pepper if necessary. Cool. In batches, put the soup in the liquidizer. Flick the motor on and off once or twice (you want a rough chopped effect, *not* a smooth purée). Serve piping hot. The soup will keep in the refrigerator for several days and may be frozen.

CHESTNUT SOUP

Serves 8
198 Calories per serving
1.4 g fat

This is a soup for special occasions, a rich starter for a gala meal. The use of tinned chestnuts (available in delicatessens and many supermarkets) makes it very easy to prepare. Happily, chestnuts, unlike other nuts, are very low in fat.

6 shallots chopped	32 fl oz/960 ml tinned unsweetened
¾ lb/338 g carrots, peeled and	chestnuts, drained
chopped	Salt and freshly ground pepper to
1 large celery stalk, chopped	taste
3 pts/1,800 ml stock	¼ teaspoon freshly grated nutmeg
8 fl oz/240 ml dry red wine	8 fl oz/240 ml skimmed milk

1   Combine the shallots, carrots, celery, 4 fl oz/120 ml of stock and 4 fl oz/120 ml of wine in a soup pot. Cover, bring to a boil, and boil until almost all the liquid is cooked away.

2   Add chestnuts, remaining stock and seasonings. Simmer, covered, for 45 minutes to 1 hour, until the chestnuts and vegetables are very tender. Cool slightly.

3   Purée in a liquidizer. Return to the soup pot and stir in the milk. Bring back to a simmer and simmer for 10 minutes. The soup may be served at once, or cooled and refrigerated for serving up to 3 days later.
4   To serve, bring to a simmer. Stir in remaining wine and simmer for a few minutes.

'There were great, round, pot-bellied baskets of chestnuts, shaped like the waistcoats of jolly old gentlemen.'

Charles Dickens, *A Christmas Carol*, 1843

ITALIAN SAUSAGE SOUP

Serves 8
191 Calories per serving
1.2 g fat
(traditional Italian sausage soup: 700 Calories, 50 g fat)

This one-pot meal is more of a stew than a soup. It provides lavish comfort on a cold, wintery evening. Eat it in front of the fire. Serve a crusty rustic wholegrain loaf with it. The soup reheats very well – in fact it improves in flavour if made a day or so ahead.

---

2 large onions, coarsely chopped
3 cloves garlic, crushed
2½ pts/1,500 ml stock
1 tin (1 lb 12 oz/784 g) plum tomatoes, drained and crushed with the hands
12 fl oz/360 ml dry red wine
1 teaspoon dried basil, crumbled
1 teaspoon dried oregano, crumbled
1 piece Parmesan cheese rind
1 small red pepper, seeded, ribbed and coarsely diced

3 small courgettes, trimmed and sliced ½ in/1.27 cm thick
2½ oz/70 g tiny pasta shells
Salt and freshly ground pepper to taste
4 tablespoons fresh parsley, chopped
1 tin (15 oz/425 g) cannelini beans, drained
25 Italian Sausage Balls, cooked (see page 94)
Grated Parmesan cheese

---

1   Sauté onions and garlic in 6 fl oz/180 ml stock according to the Slim Cuisine technique (see p. 22) until amber brown and tender. Stir in tomatoes, wine, remaining stock, herbs, and Parmesan rind. Simmer briskly, uncovered, for 15 minutes.
2   Add red pepper, courgettes, pasta, salt and pepper. Cover. Simmer for 10 minutes, or until the pasta and vegetables are tender. Stir occasionally.

3   Add parsley, sausage balls and beans. Heat through. Discard the Parmesan rind. Serve piping hot. Pass round Parmesan cheese at the table.

'Cold soup is a very tricky thing and it is the rare hostess who can carry it off. More often than not the dinner guest is left with the impression that had he only come a little earlier he could have gotten it while it was still hot.'

Fran Lebowitz, *Metropolitan Life*, 1978

CHILLED CORN SOUP

Makes 3 pts/1,800 ml
115 Calories per 10 fl oz/300 ml
0.8 g fat
(traditional corn soup: 200 Calories, 11.7 g fat)

This recipe is adapted from the Roux brothers, my gastronomic heroes. I specify a frying pan, an odd utensil for soup. But you will find that the skimmed milk is less likely to scorch and overflow in a frying pan than in a saucepan.

1 small onion, halved and sliced into thin half-moons	*Salt to taste*
	Pinch nutmeg
4 fl oz/120 ml stock	*Pinch paprika*
12 oz/336 g sweet corn kernels	*Snipped chives*
28 fl oz/840 ml skimmed milk	

1   In a non-stick frying pan sauté the onion in the stock according to the Slim Cuisine technique (see p. 22).
2   If the corn kernels are tinned, rinse and drain them. Add to the onion and stir. Pour in the milk, season with nutmeg and a bit of salt. Gently and slowly bring to a boil. Simmer for 5 minutes. Cool slightly.
3   Purée the mixture in the blender, then rub it through a sieve. Chill.
4   Serve with a sprinkling of paprika and chives on each bowlful.

Variation:

MEXICAN CORN SOUP

Add ground cumin, cayenne pepper and a pinch of crumbled dried oregano in Step 2. Omit the nutmeg. In Step 3 omit the paprika and chives. Garnish with chopped fresh coriander and a sprinkling of chilli powder.

JELLIED GAZPACHO

Serves 10
58 Calories per serving
0.1 g fat

A trembling red jelly, studded with jewel-like bits of vegetables and herbs – fragrant, vivid, and exciting. Serve it unmoulded onto greens or creamy buttermilk, or – even better – spooned into clear glass bowls. It can be eaten with a spoon or spread onto savoury biscuits.

---

1 small and 1 large tin Italian plum
   tomatoes with juice (2 lb 10 oz/
   1,176 g in all)
4 teaspoons plain gelatine
6 oz/168 g tomato paste
Juice of ½ lemon
2 fl oz/60 ml white wine vinegar
Salt and pepper to taste
Dash of cayenne pepper (optional)
1 teaspoon fresh oregano
1 teaspoon fresh basil

1 clove garlic, crushed
⅕ pt/120 ml thinly sliced spring
   onions
½ yellow pepper, chopped
¼ cucumber, peeled, seeded and
   chopped
⅕ pt/120 ml parsley, chopped
2 tinned plum tomatoes, seeded,
   well drained and chopped (in
   summer, use fresh tomatoes)

---

1   Liquidize the tomatoes, juice and all, then sieve them. You should end up with 1½ pts/900 ml of tomato juice. Save any extra for another use. Measure out 6 fl oz/180 ml and put into a non-reactive saucepan. Bring just to a simmer. Immediately remove from the heat.

2   Sprinkle the gelatine into the hot tomato juice. Stir well to dissolve. Add the remaining tomato juice, tomato paste, lemon juice, vinegar, salt, pepper and cayenne, if used. Stir very well. Let stand for an hour or so until the mixture is beginning to thicken.

3   Fold in the remaining ingredients. Pour the mixture into a mould, several small moulds or a large bowl. Cover and chill.

4   To serve, if you are using moulds, dip the bottom of each mould *very briefly* into warm water. Loosen the gelatine around the edges with a flexible palette knife. Unmould onto a bed of greens or onto a pool of buttermilk. Serve at once.

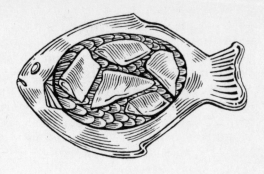

Fish

'Fish dinners will make a man spring like a flea.'
Thomas Jordan, 1640

This section deals very specifically with techniques. There are countless ways of seasoning, saucing and serving fish. Once you learn the Slim Cuisine techniques of fish cookery, let your imagination run wild.

A fish dinner is my idea of culinary heaven. The delicacy of fish and its ability to 'marry' with a large spectrum of flavourful ingredients make finny creatures my first choice of main course for special dinner parties and celebration meals. A word of warning, however. When fish is overcooked or kept several days past its prime, it is fit for no one but a not-very-fastidious cat. Fish should be sparklingly fresh and *just* cooked so that it is moist, succulent and sweetly flavourful.

Secrets of Perfect Fish Cookery

To cook fish properly, cook it quickly. Do not 'cook until it flakes easily' as many recipes direct. Instead cook it until it turns opaque and just barely begins to flake. It should retain the faint sweet taste and moisture of the sea or stream. To achieve the proper effect, follow this foolproof rule of thumb developed by the Canadian Fisheries Board: With a ruler, measure the fish at its thickest point (see illustration). Cook the fish (under a grill, in the oven or in a frying pan) at high heat for 10 minutes per in/2.5 cm thickness of fish. Thus if the fish is ½ in/1.27 cm or less thick it will cook for 5 minutes, 1½ in/3.8 cm for 15 minutes, and so on.

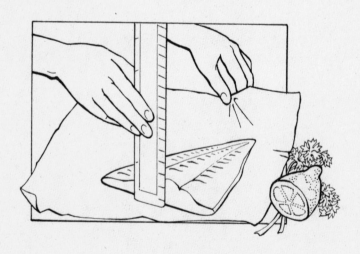

To Buy Fresh Fish

All the careful timing and exquisite seasoning in the world are useless when applied to old fish. Shop carefully and keep these points in mind:

1 If it smells fishy, forget it! Fish should have a faint, clean odour of the sea or the stream. Any trace of fishiness means old fish.
2 Fresh fish is firm. Poke it with your finger. If the flesh springs back it is fresh. If the dent remains, the fish is not for you.
3 A fish fillet should not shred or tear when held up. And fillets should never feel slimy.
4 Fish that has been stored improperly or too long develop sunken, milky, filmed eyes. Choose fish with bulging, bright, staring eyes, however unnerving that stare may be.
5 If the proprietor of the fish market does not allow you to poke, prod and smell the wares, consider finding another market.

Fish Facts

Fish makes a perfect main dish from a nutritional standpoint as well as a gastronomic one. Low in calories and sodium, high in protein and B vitamins, it is a dietitian's dream. The fat content of fish varies with the species, but even fattier fish is relatively low in calories, and fish fat is entirely different from animal fat. Recent scientific and medical studies in several different countries suggest that fish oils seem to have a protective effect on the heart. Frequent fish meals, coupled with an otherwise low-fat diet, may well help reduce the risk of heart disease.

Calorie Values for Boned Fish
(Calories per 3½ oz/100 g)

Cod	83	Lemon sole	91
Haddock	98	Salmon	197
Halibut	92	Brown trout	135
Plaice	93		

'My guest's nostrils swell out, a new light shines in his eyes and he goes after that fish as if he hadn't eaten a thing all day. He can't get over it. He praises it to the skies. He fills a glass with brandy and drinks a toast to the fish.'

Sholom Aleichem, *Tit for Tat*, 1915

Slim Cuisine Methods of Cooking Fish

Use no fats and oils and (it should go without saying) abandon all thoughts of deep frying. For the sake of good taste, avoid blanketing fish in thick tomato sauces, or excessive showerings of dried herbs. Keep it simple so that the fresh, vibrant taste of the fish itself shines through.

TO STEAM FISH IN PARCHMENT

Steaming fish *en papillote* (in paper packets) is a classic method that lends itself perfectly to Slim Cuisine. The fish steams in its own juices and emerges spectacularly succulent and luscious. Keep seasoning fresh and simple. For each piece of fish use a tablespoon of dry white wine, sherry or white vermouth, a tablespoon of lemon juice and a scattering of chopped fresh herbs. Try parsley, spring onion and minced fresh ginger; basil or mint and minced garlic; thyme, tarragon and slivered orange zest; coriander, lime juice and slivered lime zest; ginger, spring onions and soy sauce. Chopped or sliced mushrooms can be added too. Find combinations that please you and those you feed.

1   Use fish steaks, fillets, or small whole fish, such as trout, gutted and boned. (When using whole fish, remove the head and tail if desired. Some flavour will be lost with the head but you will be spared the baleful stare.) Rinse the fish and dry it on paper towels. With tweezers or a small pair of pliers, pull out any small bones that remain in the fillets or boneless whole fish.

2   With a ruler, measure the fish at its thickest point. (Be sure to measure its *depth* not its length!) Jot down the inches or centimetres of thickness.

3   For each piece of fish tear a piece of greaseproof paper large enough to enclose the piece generously. Place each portion of fish on a piece of paper (fillets should be skin side down) near the bottom edge. Season with appropriate herbs, spices, citrus juice and spirits (see suggestions above). Fold the paper over the fish. The outer edges of the paper should be even. Crimp the paper closed over the fish as follows: fold down one corner; start a second fold so that it incorporates a bit of the first fold; continue folding and crimping all around until the fish is well secured and no steam or juices can escape. Make sure you leave space on top so that the paper does not touch the top surface of the fish.

4   Preheat the oven to 450° F (230° C/Gas Mark 8). Place the fish packets, in one layer, on a baking sheet. Bake for 10 minutes per in/2.5 cm thickness of fish (see p. 78).

5   Give each diner a packet and a pair of scissors. When the packets are cut, the perfumed steam will imbue the air, delighting all present.

fold down one corner.

Start a second fold so that it incorporates a bit of the first fold.

Continue folding and crimping all around until

the fish is well secured and no steam or juice can escape.

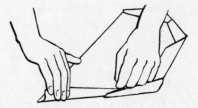

Make sure you leave space on top so that the paper does not touch the top surface of the fish.

TO GRILL FISH

Years ago when I was visiting friends in Maine on the North East Coast of the United States, I learned to coat fish fillets with a thin layer of mayonnaise before grilling, to keep them beautifully moist. It works with Slim Cuisine mayonnaise too. For fish, I make the mayonnaise with a mixture of 2 parts yoghurt to 1 part Dijon mustard. In the grilling the coating turns fluffy, and the fish stays moist and pearly.

GRILLED PLAICE WITH MUSTARD

Serves 4
84 Calories per serving
0.8 g fat

White wine	*2 tablespoons low-fat yoghurt*
4 plaice fillets	*Freshly ground pepper*
1 tablespoon Dijon mustard	

1   Preheat grill to its highest point.
2   Pour wine to a depth of $\frac{1}{16}$ in/0.15 cm into the grill pan.
3   Place the fillets in one layer in the pan. (They should not touch each other.)
4   Combine mustard, yoghurt and pepper. Spread evenly over each fillet.
5   Grill 4–5 ins/12 cm from the heat for 5 minutes. Serve at once.

TO OVEN-POACH FISH

1   Preheat the oven to 450° F (230° C/Gas Mark 8).
2   With a ruler, measure the fish at its thickest point (be sure to measure its *depth* not its length!) Jot down the inches or centimetres of thickness.
3   Pour dry white wine or dry vermouth into a shallow baking dish to a depth of $\frac{1}{16}$ in/0.15 cm. Place the fish steaks or fish fillets (skin side down) in the wine in one layer (they should not touch each other). Season to taste or as indicated in the individual recipe. The seasoning suggestions for fish *en papillote* also apply to steamed fish and to poached fish. Cover each piece of fish with a lettuce leaf. (This keeps the fish from drying out.) Bake for 10 minutes per in/2.5 cm thickness of fish. Discard lettuce leaves and serve at once.

TO OVEN-'FRY' FISH

126 Calories per 3½ oz/100 g (of cod)
0.6 g fat
(traditional fried cod: 200 Calories per 3½ oz/100 g, 10.3 g fat)

1   Preheat oven to 500° F (290° C/Gas Mark 9).
2   Choose haddock or cod fillets. With a ruler, measure the fillet at its thickest point. (Be sure to measure its *depth* not its length!) Jot down the inches or centimetres of thickness.
3   Dip one side of the fillets (not the skin side) into buttermilk or yoghurt, then dredge them in seasoned breadcrumbs. (Make your own. The packaged kind tend to be awful. Season them with salt and pepper and any herbs and spices you like.) The fish should be very well coated.
4   Place a rack on a flat baking sheet. Put the fillets, breaded side up, on the rack in one layer (they should not touch each other). Bake for 10 minutes per in/2.5 cm thickness. Serve at once with lemon wedges. This fish is particularly good on a bed of Helen's Terracotta Sauce (see page 147).

TO STEAM FISH FILLETS

Serves 4

Lettuce leaves	3 tablespoons finely minced shallots
4 fish fillets approximately 6 oz/	or thinly sliced spring onions
168 g each (white fish or salmon)	2 tablespoons chopped fresh parsley
2 tablespoons dry white wine or	1 tablespoon chopped fresh herbs
vermouth or 2 tablespoons fresh	(tarragon, thyme, marjoram or
lemon or lime juice	chervil)
	Salt and freshly ground pepper

---

1   Line a steamer rack with lettuce leaves. Arrange the fish fillets, skin side down, in one layer on the leaves. Sprinkle them evenly with all the remaining ingredients. Have water boiling in the bottom of the steamer.
2   Put the rack in the steamer, cover and steam the fish over boiling water for 10 minutes per in/2.5 cm thickness. Serve at once.

Suggestions for Steamed, Poached or 'Fried' Fish

Serve the fish fillets on a bed of:
Remoulade Sauce (see page 58)

Tzatziki (see page 57)
Red or Yellow Pepper Sauce (see page 146), or coat the plate with
half yellow pepper sauce, half red, before positioning the fish
Hungarian Green Sauce (see page 144)
Dill Pesto (see page 145)
Helen's Terracotta Sauce (see page 147)

PLAICE EN PAPILLOTE

Serves 4
95 Calories per serving
0.6 g fat

---

1 large Spanish onion, halved and sliced into paper-thin half moons	2 tablespoons chopped fresh tarragon or 1 teaspoon dried tarragon
4 fl oz/120 ml stock	
4 plaice fillets	2 tablespoons chopped chives or thinly sliced spring onions
Salt and freshly ground pepper to taste	

---

1   Preheat oven to 450° F (230° C/Gas Mark 8).
2   Sauté the onion in stock according to the Slim Cuisine method
     (see page 22) until amber brown and meltingly tender.
3   Place each fillet on a square of greaseproof paper large enough
     to enclose it. Season each with salt and pepper, and top with
     an equal amount of herbs. Put some of the sautéed onions on
     top of each fillet.
4   Seal and cook according to the master recipe (see page 80).
     Serve at once.

COD EN PAPILLOTE

Serves 4
93 Calories per serving
0.3 g fat

Here is a lovely fresh, simple way to cook cod in greaseproof-paper
packets; just one example of how this method can produce a quick
but extremely elegant main dish. Serve it with steamed new
potatoes and a green salad tossed with one of the Slim Cuisine
dressings (see page 182).

*4 cod fillets, 4 oz/112 g each (choose
    fillets that are of equal thickness)*
*4 generous tablespoons chopped
    fresh parsley*
*4 generous tablespoons chopped
    fresh mint*

4 tablespoons fresh lemon juice
4 tablespoons dry white vermouth
*Salt and freshly ground pepper to
    taste*

1   Preheat the oven to 450° F (230° C/Gas Mark 8).
2   Measure the thickness of the cod fillets. Place each fillet on a
    sheet of greaseproof paper.
3   Sprinkle a tablespoon of parsley, mint, lemon juice, ver-
    mouth, and some salt and pepper over each fillet. Enclose the
    fillets in the paper according to the directions in the master
    recipe (see page 80).
4   Place the packets on a baking sheet and bake for 10 minutes
    per in/2.5 cm thickness of fish. Serve at once, right from the
    packets.

Meat

'Vegetables are interesting, but lack a sense of
purpose when unaccompanied by a good cut of meat.'

Fran Lebowitz, *Metropolitan Life*, 1979

There is no need to cut out red meat, in fact it is wise not to. Meat is an excellent source of nutrition: high quality protein, B vitamins, zinc and other important trace minerals, iron and more. In fact, the iron from meat is absorbed more readily into the body than the iron in any other foodstuff or iron supplement. Of course, meat is also a source of fat, much of it (although not all of it) saturated. So the trick is to eliminate as much of that fat as possible.

Here are the guidelines:

1 Buy the leanest meat possible. Goose skirt for instance, a paddle-shaped flat steak, is extremely lean and makes a wonderfully satisfying steak dinner. (Ask your butcher to save this cut for you.) Beef fillet steak is lean, as is pork tenderloin. Always trim away all visible fat before cooking.

2 Rethink the *amount* of meat you eat at one meal. Serve plenty of vegetables and grains with smaller portions of meat. Do as the Chinese do, and make meat more of an accent than a main event. And there is certainly no need to eat meat every day. Eat poultry, fish, dairy and vegetarian meals as well.

3 Mince is a great favourite of mine. Some of the most comforting and delicious dishes in the world – meatballs, bolognese sauce, shepherd's pie, chilli con carne – are made with mince. Always buy *very* lean mince, whether it is beef, pork, lamb or veal. The ideal is to buy a piece of extremely lean meat from the butcher and have him mince it.

4 Never brown mince in added fat. Use a non-stick frying pan and let it brown in its own juices. Then drain it very well in a colander. Even very lean meat will have rendered plenty of fat. After draining it well, spread it out on paper towels, cover with more paper towels, and blot. Blot out the frying pan. Then, when all possible fat has been removed, return the meat to the pan and proceed with the recipe.

5 Stews are disastrous when made from very lean meat. Use beef chuck, and trim off surrounding fat. Never brown the meat cubes in fat or oil when beginning a stew. Simply combine the ingredients and braise slowly and gently. During stewing, the meat cubes will have released lots of fat. Refrigerate the stew overnight, or quick chill the juices in the freezer. The fat will rise to the top and harden. Scrape off every speck and discard it.

Meatballs

Tiny, succulent meatballs are delightful. Traditional meatballs are horrendously high in Calories and fat, but it is easy to remedy this. Slim Cuisine techniques result in meatballs that are much more delicate and refined than those made by the bad old methods. In fact, they are more like light and fluffy dumplings than meatballs. Instead of eggs (the yolk is extremely high fat), baked, puréed aubergine is combined with the minced meat. 'Wait!' I hear you exclaim. 'What about those of us who loathe aubergine?' Stay calm. There is no taste, no look, no evidence whatsoever of aubergine in the final cooked meatballs. The vegetable pulp imparts an exquisite lightness, but otherwise there is no sign of that pulp at all.

Instead of frying the meatballs in olive oil, butter or other highly unsuitable fat, Slim Cuisine calls for quick grilling, or sautéing in stock. The choice is yours and both methods will work beautifully for lamb, beef or pork. Traditional meatball recipes call for fairly high-fat minced meat. Obviously for these recipes you will use the leanest meat possible.

GRILLED LAMB MEATBALLS

Makes 35 nut-sized meatballs
18 Calories per meatball
0.3 g fat
(traditional meatballs: 88.2 calories per meatball, 5. g fat)

Good in Tomato Sauce, a lovely addition to pasta dishes, splendid with Steamed Asparagus and Red or Yellow Pepper Sauce (see page 161 or 146), or try them stuffed into pitta bread with Stir-'Fried' Peppers (see page 162) or Raita (see page 183).

---

1 lb/450 g lean minced lamb
1 small aubergine (¾–1 lb/450 g) baked and puréed or chopped fine (see page 32)
3 cloves garlic, minced
¼ pt/150 ml fresh chopped mint (for a variation, substitute ½ tablespoon fennel seeds, or 1 tablespoon grated fresh ginger, or ¼ pt/150 ml fresh chopped coriander)

¼ pt/150 ml fresh chopped parsley
1 rounded tablespoon tomato paste
Juice and grated rind of 1 small lemon
⅕ pt/120 ml breadcrumbs
Salt and freshly ground pepper to taste

---

1   Place minced lamb in a bowl. Add remaining ingredients. Mix with your hands until thoroughly amalgamated. Fry a tiny test piece (use no fat!) in a small, non-stick frying pan. Taste, then adjust seasonings in the meat mixture to your liking.
2   Preheat the grill to its highest setting.
3   With your hands roll small balls, each a little smaller than a walnut. You will have approximately 35 in all. Line the grill pan with foil, shiny side up. Put a rack on the grill pan. Place the meatballs on the rack.
4   When the grill is very hot, grill the meatballs, 1 in/2.5 cm from the heat, for 5–7 minutes until browned on top and *just* cooked through (no need to turn them). Remove very gently using tongs and a spatula. Blot on paper towels to eliminate any faint trace of fat, and serve. The meatballs may be made in advance and refrigerated. To reheat, place them in a shallow frying pan with some warm stock. Simmer gently, covered, for 5–7 minutes. (Don't boil. The surface of the stock should barely move.) Fish out very gently with a slotted spoon.

SAUTÉED VEAL MEATBALLS

Makes 35 meatballs
23 Calories per meatball
0.5 g fat

Elegant, delicate and exquisite. Sautéing in stock is more difficult and fussy than grilling, but it is worth the effort. Of course, you can grill these if you wish.

1 lb/450 g lean minced veal	2 tablespoons chopped fresh parsley
1 small aubergine (¾–1 lb/450 g) baked and puréed or chopped fine (see page 32)	Salt and freshly ground pepper to taste
baked from 1 head of garlic (see page 29)	Juice and grated rind of 1 small lemon
1 rounded tablespoon tomato paste	6 tablespoons freshly grated Parmesan cheese
⅕ pt/120 ml dry breadcrumbs	Chicken stock

1   Combine all ingredients except chicken stock. Use your hands to mix it all gently but thoroughly. Fry a tiny piece in a non-stick frying pan (use no fat!) and taste. Adjust seasonings to your liking.
2   Form the mixture into balls that are a bit smaller than walnuts. Heat a large, heavy, non-stick frying pan. Pour in some stock

90

to just film the bottom. Put in some veal balls. Do not crowd them. Do in several batches.

3   Let them get crusty, loosening with a spatula and turning with tongs so that they brown on all sides. (Be gentle, they are fragile.) When they are browned and crusty all over add a bit more stock and simmer for 2–3 minutes, turning them, until just cooked through. Blot on paper towels, then spread them in a wide, shallow dish. Repeat until all the meat is used. Add more stock as needed. When all the veal balls are done, cover well with cling film, and refrigerate until needed. (They may be prepared to this point three days ahead.)

4   To serve, pour ½ in/1.27 cm of stock into a deep, non-stick frying pan. Add the veal balls in one layer. Cover and simmer for 10 minutes or so, until heated through.

Note: To grill the veal meatballs, follow the directions for grilling the lamb meatballs with this difference: grill for 4 minutes, turn *very* carefully (they are quite fragile) and grill for approximately 4 minutes on the second side.

MEXICAN FRIJOL-ALBONDIGA CASSEROLE

Serves 6
212 Calories per serving
2.3 g fat

Mexican baked beans with spicy meatballs. For a lively dinner party serve this dish with Chilaquiles (see page 129), Steamed Rice, and Lime-Cumin Courgettes (see page 159). Begin with Jellied Gazpacho or Chilled Corn Soup and end with Mango Sorbet.

Beans
Makes 1¼ pts/750 ml

1 large onion, chopped	1 tin (1 lb/450 g) canellini beans,
2 large cloves garlic, crushed	drained and rinsed
½ teaspoon dried oregano,	1 tin (1 lb/450 g) haricots blanc,
crumbled	drained and rinsed
½ teaspoon chilli powder	1 tinned green chilli, chopped
¾ teaspoon ground cumin	1 tin (1 lb/450 g) chopped tomatoes
6 fl oz/ 180 ml stock	2 tablespoons chopped parsley
1 teaspoon Dijon mustard	Salt to taste

1   In a large frying pan combine the onion, garlic, herbs and spices and stock. Boil until the mixture is almost dry.

91

2   Stir in the mustard, beans, chopped chilli, tomatoes, parsley and salt. Simmer gently, stirring occasionally, for 15–20 minutes until thick.

Albondigas
Makes 38 meatballs

---

1 lb/450 g very lean minced veal or pork	*1 tablespoon fresh mint or coriander, chopped*
Pulp from 1 (¾–1 lb/450 g) baked aubergine, peeled and chopped (see page 32)	*½ teaspoon cumin*
	Salt and freshly ground pepper to taste
2 spring onions, chopped	*Juice and grated rind of ½ lime*
⅕ pt/120 ml dry wholewheat breadcrumbs	*1 tablespoon tomato paste*
	2 tinned green chillies, minced
	Several dashes tabasco sauce

---

1   Preheat grill. Line the grill tray with foil, shiny side up. Place the grill rack on the tray.
2   Combine all meatball ingredients in a bowl. Mix well with the hands until well blended. Fry a tiny piece in a small non-stick frying pan (use no fat!) and taste. Adjust seasonings to your taste.
3   Form the mixture into tiny balls, a little smaller than walnuts, and arrange on the grill rack. Grill close to the heat for four minutes on each side.

To Assemble

Stock
1 tablespoon Parmesan cheese

---

1   Preheat oven to 350° F (180° C/Gas Mark 4).
2   Spread the beans on the bottom of a shallow baking dish. Add enough stock to make a slightly soupy mixture. Place albondigas on the bean mixture, pushing them in as you do so. Sprinkle the Parmesan cheese over everything. Cover the dish.
3   Bake for 30–35 minutes, until hot and bubbly.

KOFTA CURRY

Serves 4 (31 meatballs)
148 Calories per serving
1.9 g fat
(traditional kofta curry: 591 Calories per serving, 42.8 g fat)

Little meatballs, how I love them! Remember the Slim Cuisine technique of adding chopped, roasted aubergine to the meat. There will be no aubergine taste but the calories in each meatball will be reduced, and the meatballs will be tender and juicy even though the meat is very lean. Of all the curry recipes developed for this book, my tasters loved this one the best. It reheats well from both the refrigerator and the freezer.

Meatballs

2–3 cloves garlic, minced
Pulp from 1 baked aubergine (see page 32)
1 lb/450 g very lean ground lamb (lean beef can be used too, if desired)
½ teaspoon ground cinnamon

Pinch ground cloves
½ tablespoon fresh ginger root, finely grated
Salt to taste
¼ pint/150 ml fresh coriander or parsley, chopped

Sauce

2 large onions, cut into eighths
16 fl oz/480 ml stock
2 cloves garlic, minced
½ teaspoon ground turmeric
½ teaspoon ground cinnamon

2 teaspoons ground coriander
Pinch cayenne pepper (or to taste)
3 tablespoons tomato paste
Salt to taste

1   Preheat the grill to its highest setting.
2   In a large bowl, combine the meatball ingredients. Mix with your hands until thoroughly amalgamated. Fry a tiny piece in a small frying pan (use no fat!) and taste. Adjust seasonings to your liking. Form the mixture into small balls, a little smaller than walnuts.
3   Line the grill tray with foil, shiny side up. Place a rack on the tray and arrange the meatballs on it. Grill, 1 in/2.5 cm from the heat, for 5 minutes, until crusty brown on top. Set aside.
4   Separate the segments of the onion pieces. Spread them in a heavy, non-reactive frying pan. Add *no* liquid or fat. Heat the frying pan gently. Cook at moderate heat, without stirring, for 7–10 minutes, until the onions are sizzling, and beginning to stick to the pan.
5   Stir in 10 fl oz/300 ml of stock and let it bubble up, stirring up the browned deposits with a wooden spoon as it bubbles. Stir in the spices. Simmer gently, stirring all the while, until the mixture is very thick (not at all soupy). Don't rush this step, as

it is essential that the spices cook properly. Taste the mixture. The spices should not have a raw, harsh taste. Cook very gently for a few more minutes if necessary.

6   Stir in the tomato paste and the remaining (6 fl oz) stock. Place the meatballs in this sauce. Simmer gently, covered, for 15–20 minutes, until the sauce is very thick and rich. Serve at once or cool and refrigerate until needed. This tastes good on the second or third day so do not hesitate to make in advance. Add more stock when reheating.

ITALIAN SAUSAGE BALLS

Makes 35 sausage balls
25 Calories per sausage ball
0.2 g fat
(traditional Italian sausage: 105 Calories per ounce, 8 g fat)

Sausage is a savoury mixture of minced pork and pork fat stuffed into animal intestine casings. The seasonings change with the type of sausage and the region of its birth: nutmeg and mace for German bratwurst; marjoram and garlic for Polish keilbasa; garlic and red pepper for Spanish chorizo; cinnamon, allspice and orange peel for Greek loukanika; sage and thyme for English butcher's sausage.

Use the technique for Slim Cuisine Meatballs to produce juicy, well-flavoured sausage meat without the fat. Pork is bred to be leaner and leaner these days. It should be no problem obtaining a lean piece at the butcher. Have him mince it for you. Or buy lean pork mince from the supermarket. Instead of stuffing the sausage mixture into casings, form it into balls and grill. Even though the meat is lean, it still has some fat in it, which drips off nicely in the grilling. This recipe is for one of my favourites; Italian sausage with crushed dried chillies and fennel seeds. Substitute any seasonings you like to produce *your* favourite sausages. And, if you wish, make your sausages with beef or veal, or a combination of meats.

---

1 lb/450 g minced lean pork	3 garlic cloves, crushed to a paste
3 small aubergines (approx.	with a mallet
¾ lb/340 g each) baked, skinned	4 tablespoons parsley, finely
and puréed in the liquidizer (see	chopped
page 32)	3 tablespoons dry red wine
1 teaspoon fennel or anise seeds	Salt and freshly ground pepper to
¼ teaspoon crushed dried chillies	taste

---

1   Combine all ingredients and mix very well until thoroughly amalgamated. Fry a tiny test piece (use no fat!) in a small, non-stick frying pan. Taste, then adjust seasonings in the meat mixture to your liking.
2   Preheat grill to its highest setting.
3   With your hands, roll small balls, each a little smaller than a walnut. Line the grill pan with foil, shiny side up. Put a rack on the grill pan. Place the sausage balls on the rack.
4   When the grill is very hot, grill the sausage balls, 1 in/2.5 cm from the heat, for 5 minutes. Turn and grill for 2 minutes on the second side. Blot on paper towels to remove any trace of fat. Refrigerate until needed. Reheat in stock (see page 90).

Sausage Ideas

Combine the Italian Sausages with Grilled or Stir- 'Fried' Peppers (see pages 162–3), Sautéed Mushrooms (see page 26) and Tomato Sauce (see page 151) and serve with pasta, or stuffed into crusty rolls. Italian Sausages in Tomato Sauce freeze very well.

Serve Sausage Balls with mashed potatoes and browned onions (see page 23).

Serve Sausage Balls with Sautéed Mushrooms (see page 26) and grilled tomatoes. What a breakfast!

> 'If there's an end
> On which I'd spend
> My last remaining cash
> It's sausage, friend
> It's sausage, friend,
> It's sausage, friend, and mash.'

> Sir A. P. Herbert, 1925

Mince

I'd rather have mince than steak. When I'm hungry for 'home cooking', for something warm and comforting and evocative of happy childhood days, give me mince everytime. It's amazing the interesting things you can do with it. The following collection of recipes covers the UK, India, the USA and Italy.

HAMBURGERS

Makes 4 generous burgers
161 Calories per burger
2.5 g fat
(traditional hamburger: 330 Calories, 23 g fat)

Imagine a huge hamburger – juicy and meaty – festooned with shreds of caramelized onions and doused in a thick, spicy red sauce, nestling between the halves of a wheaty bun. Sounds marvellous, but quite forbidden, doesn't it? Not to worry. The Slim Cuisine Burger is even juicier and more flavourful than the fattening original.

---

12 oz/336 g fine lean minced beef
3 tablespoons crisp wholemeal
   breadcrumbs
1 scant tablespoon tomato paste
2 teaspoons low-fat fromage blanc
   or yoghurt
2 tablespoons Parmesan cheese
1 small onion, chopped fine

1 (¾–1 lb/450 g) aubergine,
   roasted, peeled and coarsely
   chopped
1–2 cloves garlic, minced
Salt and freshly ground pepper to
   taste
2 tablespoons additional crisp
   wholemeal breadcrumbs

---

1   Preheat the grill to its highest temperature. Place the grill shelf on its lowest position. Line the grill tray with foil, shiny side up. Place the grill rack on the tray.
2   Thoroughly mix together all ingredients except the additional breadcrumbs. Shape the mixture into 4 fat, oval cakes. Dredge them, on both sides, in the additional crumbs.
3   Grill on the rack in the lowest position for 3–4 minutes on each side, until crusty on the outside and medium rare within. (Cook more or less to your taste, but please don't incinerate them!)
4   Serve as they are, or in wholewheat buns with Browned Onions and Red Pepper Sauce. Or serve with a dollop of Pesto on each burger.

*Rajmaa (page 137) is a zesty
Indian mixture of red beans and spicy onions.
Farmer's omelette (page 136): a satisfying,
old-fashioned open-faced 'pie' of browned potatoes
and eggs with a touch of cheese.*

SHEPHERD'S PIE

Serves 8
211 Calories per serving
3.2 g fat
(traditional shepherd's pie 357 Calories, 23 g fat)

This pie is for a slim and healthy shepherd. Many changes can be rung on this familiar theme. See suggestions below.

---

2 lb/900 g lean minced lamb (beef or
   veal may be used as well)
3 onions, finely chopped
3 cloves garlic, minced
½ pt/300 ml stock
½ pt/300 ml dry red wine
1 tablespoon reduced-salt
   Worcestershire sauce
2 tablespoons tomato paste

Salt and freshly ground pepper to
   taste
Dash nutmeg
Well-seasoned mashed potatoes
   made from 2 lb/900 g potatoes
   and 4 fl oz/120 ml buttermilk
   (about 2 pts/1,200 ml mashed
   potatoes)
6 tablespoons Parmesan cheese

---

1   Cook the lamb in a large non-stick frying pan, breaking up the lumps as it cooks. When the lamb is cooked through, drain it well in a colander. Spread it out on paper towels and blot it with more paper towels. Wash and dry the frying pan. Return the drained and blotted lamb to the pan.

2   Meanwhile, combine onion, garlic, 5 fl oz/150 ml stock and 5 fl oz/150 ml wine in a non-reactive frying pan. Simmer briskly, stirring occasionally until the onions are tender and the liquid is almost gone. Add this mixture to the drained lamb.

3   Stir in the Worcestershire sauce, tomato paste, salt and peppers. Stir in remaining stock and wine. Simmer uncovered for 20–30 minutes, stirring occasionally, until thick. Taste and adjust seasonings.

4   Spread the meat mixture in a gratin pan or in individual casseroles. Season the potatoes with nutmeg, and spread them over the meat. Sprinkle evenly with Parmesan cheese. At this point the pie may be covered tightly with cling film and refrigerated for 2 days. Bring to room temperature before proceeding.

A selection of rich and exciting pasta sauces:
clockwise from top left: pesto (page 145); lemon cream sauce (page 150),
bolognese sauce (page 102); Hungarian green sauce (page 144).

5   Preheat oven to 375°F (190°C/Gas Mark 5). Bake the pie uncovered, for 30–40 minutes, until browned and bubbly. Serve at once or cool, wrap tightly and freeze for a later meal. Reheat, covered, from the frozen state, either in the oven or the microwave.

Variations:

MEXICAN-STYLE SHEPHERD'S PIE

Use beef, pork or a combination. When you cook the onions in Step 2, add 1 tablespoon chilli powder, 1 teaspoon crumbled dried oregano, ¼ teaspoon ground cinnamon, ½ teaspoon ground cumin, and ½ teaspoon crushed chillis. Omit the Worcestershire sauce in Step 3. Season the mashed potato with a pinch or 2 of ground cumin and ground cayenne.

GREEK-STYLE SHEPHERD'S PIE

When you cook the onions in Step 2, add 1 teaspoon cinnamon and ½ teaspoon crumbled oregano. Omit the Worcestershire sauce in Step 3, but add the pulp of a baked aubergine (see page 32). Season the mashed potatoes with a pinch or two of cinnamon and some baked garlic purée (see page 30).

HUNTER'S PIE

Serves 6
289 Calories per serving
3 g fat

Venison is available in British markets from October to early April. It is lean as can be. During its short season try this delicate variation on the Shepherd's Pie theme.

1½ lb/680 g lean minced venison
2 carrots, finely chopped
2 onions, finely chopped
3 cloves garlic, minced
½ teaspoon dried thyme, crumbled
½ pt/300 ml dry red wine
½ pt/300 ml stock
1 tablespoon cornflour
2 tablespoons redcurrant jelly
1 tablespoon reduced-salt Worcestershire sauce

2 teaspoons lemon juice
1½ tablespoons tomato paste
Salt and freshly ground pepper to taste
Pinch cayenne pepper
Well-seasoned mashed potatoes made from 2 lb/900 g potatoes and 4 fl oz/150 ml buttermilk (see page 177)
4 tablespoons Parmesan cheese

---

1   Cook venison in a large non-stick frying pan until it has lost its redness. Break up the lumps with a wooden spoon as it cooks. When it is cooked, drain well in a colander to remove any rendered fat. Spread out on paper towels and blot it with more paper towels. Return the meat to the frying pan.

2   Meanwhile combine carrots, onion, garlic, thyme, 5 fl oz/150 ml wine and 5 fl oz/150 ml stock in a non-reactive frying pan. Simmer briskly, stirring occasionally, until the vegetables are tender and the liquid is almost gone. Add this mixture to the venison.

3   Place cornflour, jelly, Worcestershire sauce, lemon juice and tomato paste in a liquidizer and blend. Stir the mixture into the venison. Stir in the remaining wine and stock. Season with salt, pepper and cayenne. Simmer uncovered for 20–30 minutes, until thick. Stir occasionally. Taste and adjust seasonings, adding salt, peppers, Worcestershire sauce or lemon juice to your taste.

4   Spread the meat mixture in a gratin pan or in individual casseroles. Spread the mashed potatoes over the meat. Sprinkle evenly with Parmesan cheese. At this point, the pie may be refrigerated for up to 2 days. Bring to room temperature before continuing.

5   Preheat oven to 375° F (190° C/Gas Mark 5). Bake pie uncovered for 35–40 minutes, until browned and bubbly. Serve at once, or cool, cover tightly and freeze for a later meal. Reheat, covered, from the frozen state, either in the oven or the microwave.

CURRIED MINCE WITH POTATOES – KEEMA CURRY

Serves 6
179 Calories per serving
1.6 g fat
(traditional keema curry: 448 Calories per serving, 28.8 g fat)

An Indian homestyle dish that sticks to the ribs. Make sure that your mince is very lean. Keema reheats well from both the refrigerator and the freezer. In fact, it improves with keeping.

2 medium onions cut into eighths
20 fl oz/600 ml stock
2 teaspoons fresh peeled ginger, minced
2 cloves garlic, minced
1 teaspoon ground cinnamon
1 teaspoon ground coriander
Pinch ground cloves
½ teaspoon cayenne pepper
½ teaspoon ground allspice
6 whole green cardamom pods, lightly crushed

1 dried bay leaf, broken in half
1 green chilli, stemmed, seeded and minced
2 medium boiling potatoes, cut into 1 in/2.5 cm dice
3 tablespoons tomato paste
Salt and freshly ground pepper to taste
1½ lb/680 g very lean minced beef
1 tin (12 oz) chopped tomatoes
1 teaspoon garam masala

1   Separate the segments of the onion pieces and spread them in a heavy, non-stick, frying pan, Add *no* liquid or fat. Heat the frying pan gently. Cook at moderate heat, without stirring, for 7–10 minutes, until the onions are sizzling, speckled with dark amber, and beginning to stick to the pan.

2   Stir in 10 fl oz/300 ml of stock and let it bubble up, stirring up the browned deposits in the pan with a wooden spoon as it bubbles. Stir in the ginger, garlic, spices and chilli. Turn the heat down a bit and simmer, stirring frequently, until the mixture is very thick (not at all soupy), and the onions and spices are 'frying' in their own juices. Don't rush this step, as it is essential that the spices should not have a raw, harsh taste. Taste. Cook very gently for a few more minutes if necessary.

3   Toss the potatoes in the spice mixture until they are well coated. Stir in the tomato paste. Season to taste.

4   In another frying pan, cook the meat until it loses its red colour. Break it up with a wooden spoon as it cooks. Drain well in a colander. Spread out on paper towels and blot with more paper towels to eliminate even more fat. Stir the meat into the onion-potato mixture.

5   Stir in the remaining 10 oz/300 ml of stock and the tomatoes. Bring to a boil. Reduce heat and simmer briskly for about 30 minutes, uncovered, until the mixture is thick. Cover and simmer for 15 minutes more, until the potatoes are done. If at any time the mixture threatens to stick and burn stir in a bit more stock. Stir in the garam masala.

CHILLI CON CARNE

Serves 6
181 Calories per serving
1.7 g fat

This is a real Texas Chilli, with one difference – a real Texan would never stir the beans in with the meat, he would eat them on the side. If you wish, add chopped red, green and yellow peppers to the onions and spices in Step 2. It's not traditional, but it's *good*.

---

2 large onions, coarsely chopped
16 fl oz/480 ml stock
2 cloves garlic, crushed
2 tablespoons chilli powder
1 teaspoon ground cumin
1 teaspoon dried oregano, crumbled
1 teaspoon crushed chilli, optional
  (use depending on the strength
  of the chilli powder and your
  taste)

1½ lb/680 g very lean minced beef
4 tablespoons tomato paste
Salt and freshly ground pepper to
  taste
1 tin (15 oz) red kidney beans,
  drained and rinsed

---

1   Separate the segments of the onion pieces and spread them in a heavy, non-stick, frying pan. Add *no* liquid or fat. Heat the frying pan gently. Cook at moderate heat, without stirring, for 7–10 minutes, until the onions are sizzling, speckled with dark amber, and beginning to stick to the pan.
2   Stir in 10 fl oz/300 ml of stock and let it bubble up, stirring up the browned deposits in the pan with a wooden spoon as it bubbles. Stir in the garlic and spices. Turn the heat down a bit and simmer, stirring frequently, until the mixture is very thick (not at all soupy), and the onions and spices are 'frying' in their own juices. Don't rush this step, as it is essential that the spices should not have a raw, harsh taste. Taste. Cook very gently for a few more minutes if necessary.
3   In another non-stick frying pan, cook the meat until it loses its red colour. Break it up with a wooden spoon as it cooks. When the meat is thoroughly cooked, drain *very* well in a colander. Spread out on paper towels and blot with more paper towels to eliminate even more fat.
4   Combine the meat and the onion mixture. Stir in the tomato paste, the beans and enough remaining stock to just cover the contents of the pan. Add salt and pepper to taste. Bring to the simmer. Simmer, uncovered, until the mixture is thick, about ½ an hour. This freezes well.

BOLOGNESE SAUCE

makes 2½ pts/1,500 ml – serves 10
55 Calories per serving
0.4 g fat
(traditional bolognese sauce: 208 Calories per serving, 16 g fat)

Everyone loves bolognese sauce. This version stretches a small amount of meat into a sumptuous amount of sauce. It's good on all types of pasta. Consider unusual shapes as well as the standard ones. My assistant, Penny Roseveare, served the sauce with cous-cous, and it was a wonderful combination. And at a buffet I attended, June Brown dispensed with pasta altogether and served it on a bed of braised carrot slices. Brilliant!

½ lb/226 g very lean minced beef
1 medium onion, chopped
2 large cloves of garlic, crushed
1 small red pepper, chopped
1 small yellow pepper, chopped
2 tins (1 lb/450 g each) chopped
 tomatoes
4 heaped tablespoons tomato paste
2 in/5 cm piece of Parmesan cheese
 rind

Salt and freshly ground pepper to
 taste
1 tablespoon chopped fresh oregano
 (¼ teaspoon dried)
1 tablespoon chopped fresh basil (¼
 teaspoon dried)
½ lb/225 g button mushrooms,
 quartered
4 fl oz/120 ml dry red wine
4 fl oz/120 ml stock
Several dashes soy sauce

---

1   Cook the beef and onion in a non-stick, heavy frying pan over medium heat. As it browns, break up any lumps with a wooden spoon. When the meat is almost browned, stir in the garlic and the peppers. Continue to stir and cook until the meat is completely cooked through and the onions are limp. Dump the mixture into a colander to drain away any fat. Spread it out on paper towels and blot with more paper towels. Return to the frying pan.

2   Add the chopped tomatoes, tomato paste, Parmesan rind, salt, pepper and herbs. Cover the frying pan and simmer for 15 minutes.

3   Meanwhile, put the mushrooms, wine, stock and soy sauce into a non-reactive, non-stick heavy frying pan. Stir to combine everything very well. Simmer, stirring occasionally, until the liquid is almost gone. Let the mushrooms 'fry' gently in their own juices for a few moments. Do not let them scorch or stick. Add the mushrooms to the sauce.

4   Season the sauce to taste and simmer, partially covered, for

approximately ten minutes more, until thick. The sauce may be refrigerated for a day or so or frozen. Serve with pasta, or as a filling for baked potatoes.

BEEF STEW

Serves 12
160 Calories per serving
1.7 g fat
(traditional beef stew: 238 Calories per serving, 15 g fat)

A good beef stew cannot be made with extra lean meat. In the finished stew, cubes of such meat will be as dry as dust. Choose well-marbled slabs of chuck steak. This recipe shows you how to use the fat marbling in the chuck to advantage. As the stew braises, the fat and the gelatine melt out of the meat leaving it very tender. Then all of the fat rendered from the meat is meticulously removed, leaving a rich, but low-fat gravy. I sent samples of this stew to a laboratory for analysis, to assure myself that the fat really was eliminated. Raw chuck braising steak contains 9.4 per cent fat, the finished recipe only 1.75!

3 lb/1,350 g very well trimmed chuck steak, cut into ¾ in/1.9 cm cubes	1 medium floury potato, peeled and cut into ½ in/1.3 cm dice (King Edward potatoes work well here)
½ teaspoon dried thyme	Salt and freshly ground pepper to taste
1 bay leaf, crumbled	
2 fl oz/60 ml brandy	1 lb/450 g button mushrooms, quartered
12 fl oz/360 ml red wine	
2 cloves garlic, crushed	4 fl oz/120 ml red wine
16 fl oz/480 ml beef stock	4 fl oz/120 ml chicken stock
3 carrots, peeled and sliced	1 tablespoon soy sauce
3 onions, cut in half and sliced into thin half-moons	

1   Combine the beef, thyme, bay leaf, brandy, wine and garlic in a plastic bag and close tightly. Allow to marinade for at least an hour, turning the bag occasionally. If you wish, refrigerate and leave overnight.
2   Preheat oven to 350° F (180° C/Gas Mark 4).
3   Strain the marinade into a saucepan. Add beef stock. Boil until reduced by about ⅓. Skim off all foam and scum as it boils.
4   Combine the beef, carrots, onions, potato, salt and pepper in a heavy, non-reactive casserole. Cover tightly and bake for 2½ hours or until the beef is tender. Adjust the oven temperature

down during the cooking time to maintain a gentle simmer. It must not boil.

5   Dump the stew into a sieve set over a large bowl. Cover the meat and vegetables well so that they do not dry out. Pour the juices into a glass jug and place in the freezer.

6   Put the mushrooms, wine, stock and soy sauce in a non-stick frying pan. Simmer until the mushrooms are almost tender and the liquid greatly reduced. Season to taste.

7   When the stew juices in the freezer are thoroughly chilled, the fat will have risen to the top and congealed on the surface. Scrape off and discard every bit of the fat. In the stew pot combine the defatted juices and the mushrooms with their juice. Bring to a boil. Stir in the meat and vegetables. Simmer for a few minutes for the flavours to blend.

8   Mash a few potato pieces against the side of the pot and then stir. The crushed potatoes will thicken the stew. Taste and adjust the seasonings to your liking. The stew may be refrigerated for a day or two before serving. The flavour improves.

BEEF IN RED WINE

Serves 10
169 Calories per serving
2 g fat
(traditional *boeuf bourguignonne*: 907 Calories per serving, 70 g fat)

This is a simplified, low-fat, drastically Calorie-reduced version of *boeuf bourguignonne*.

3 large Spanish onions, chopped	*3 lb/1,350 g very well trimmed*
18 fl oz/540 ml chicken stock	*chuck steak, cut into ¾ in/*
6 fl oz/180 ml dry red wine	*1.9 cm cubes*
1 lb/450 g mushrooms, quartered	*1 tablespoon tomato paste*
Several dashes of soy sauce	*Salt and freshly ground pepper to*
½ teaspoon dried thyme	*taste*
½ teaspoon dried tarragon	*6 cloves garlic, halved*

1   Preheat the oven to 350° F (180° C/Gas Mark 4).
2   Combine onions and 12 fl oz/360 ml stock in a heavy non-reactive frying pan. Cover and boil for about 5 minutes. Uncover and simmer briskly until tender, browned, thick and syrupy. Raise the heat, pour in 2 fl oz/60 ml wine and boil until the alcohol has evaporated and the onions are a deep amber brown. Purée half the mixture. Combine puréed and unpuréed mixture. Set aside.

3   Combine the mushrooms, 6 fl oz/180 ml stock, 4 fl oz/120 ml wine, soy sauce and herbs in a heavy, non-reactive frying pan. Simmer briskly, stirring occasionally, until the mushrooms are tender and the liquid just about absorbed. Do not let the mushrooms scorch.

4   Combine the meat cubes with the mushrooms and onions in a baking dish. Add tomato paste, salt and pepper, and stir so that everything is well combined. Bury the garlic pieces in the stew. Bake in the oven, covered, for ½ an hour. Lower the heat to 300° F (150° C/Gas Mark 2) and cook for another 2–2½ hours, or until the meat is very tender. Adjust oven temperature down if necessary, to keep stew at a very gentle simmer.

5   Drain, saving the juices. Cover the meat well to prevent it drying out. Chill the juices in the freezer until the fat rises to the top and hardens. Discard fat. Recombine meat and juices. Refrigerate or freeze until needed.

BEEFSTEAK ON A BED OF ONIONS WITH RED PEPPER SAUCE

Serves 4
203 Calories per serving
2 g fat

This is easy and spectacular; graphic proof that low-fat, low-Calorie food does not have to be dull and austere. Serve this to very special guests at a very special occasion. There is no need to babble about the low Calorie and fat levels. If you don't tell, no one will have an inkling that this is diet food.

---

8 centre-cut fillet steaks, each about ½ in/1.3 cm thick.	4 fl oz/120 ml dry red wine
Freshly ground pepper	1 batch Red Pepper Sauce (see page 146)
1 bunch trimmed, sliced spring onions	1 batch Browned Onions (see page 23), heated to sizzling point
4 tablespoons fresh parsley, chopped	

---

1   Preheat the oven to 200° F (110° C/Gas Mark 1).
2   Trim the steaks of any vestige of fat. Trim them into neat rounds.
3   Spread a sheet of greaseproof paper on your work surface. Sprinkle lavishly with freshly ground pepper. Place steaks on the paper. Grind lots more pepper on top of the steaks. Cover with another sheet of paper. With a kitchen mallet, gently pound the meat.

4   Heat a non-stick frying pan until hot. Place the steaks in the pan so that they are not touching each other. (Do in two batches if necessary.) Cook over high heat on one side for 2–3 minutes. Turn and cook on the second side for 2–3 minutes. At this point the steaks will be nicely browned on the outside and juicy and pink within. Remove with tongs to a platter and cover loosely with foil. Put them in the oven to keep warm.

5   Scrape the spring onions and parsley into the frying pan and pour in the wine. Boil, stirring and scraping with a wooden spatula to loosen all the browned bits, until almost all the liquid is gone. Reduce heat and stir in the red pepper sauce. Pour in any juices that have collected under the meat. Stir and cook for a few minutes.

6   Spread the browned onions out onto a warm platter. Overlap the steaks on the bed of onions. Pour a ribbon of pepper sauce down the length of the meat. Serve at once. Pass the rest of the sauce in a gravy boat.

Variations:

Use Pan-Sautéed Chicken Breasts (see page 114) or Steamed Fish Fillets (see page 83) instead of beef fillet.

Goose Skirt Steak

Talk to your butcher. Smile at him. Reason with him. Ask him, most politely, to save the goose skirts for you. What a remarkable cut of meat: extremely lean, deeply flavourful, economical, and – if you cook it rare or medium-rare – very tender. Grill goose skirt or pan-sauté it without fat. Let it rest for 5–10 minutes for the juices to redistribute and then slice it thin, against the grain. Goose skirt satisfies steak cravings without guilt, and because of the way it is served – sliced thin and lavished with sautéed mushrooms or onions or a Slim Cuisine sauce – a little goes a long way.

FIVE SPICE STEAK

Serves 6
83 Calories per serving
1 g fat

Five spice powder is a fragrant Chinese mix of spices. Many supermarkets now stock it, but if you can't find it make your own with equal parts of ground cinnamon, fennel, star anise, cloves and ginger.

1 tablespoon ginger root, coarsely chopped	2 fl oz/60 ml reduced-salt Worcestershire sauce
4 large garlic cloves	½ tablespoon sugar
1½ teaspoons five spice powder	1 strip (3 in/7.6 cm × 1 in/
16 fl oz/480 ml water	2.5 cm) orange zest
4 fl oz/120 ml sherry	1 goose skirt steak (approx. 1 lb/ 450 g)

1 In a non-reactive pan, simmer all ingredients except steak for 15 minutes.
2 Put the steak in a shallow, non-reactive dish and pour marinade over it. Marinate for ½ hour or more, turning occasionally.
3 Preheat grill to highest setting. Cook steak 3 ins/7.6 cms from heat for 4–5 minutes each side (for rare).
4 Let meat rest for 3–4 minutes. Slice thinly against the grain and serve.

PEPPERED STEAK WITH MUSHROOM SAUCE

Serves 6
113 Calories per serving
1.3 g fat

A zesty preparation for goose skirt. The mushroom sauce has echoes of both Mexico and New Orleans.

1 goose skirt (approx. 1 lb/450 g)	½ teaspoon dried oregano, crumbled
Freshly ground pepper to taste	
Salt to taste	2 tinned plum tomatoes, drained and chopped
1 medium onion, finely chopped	
1 small carrot, finely chopped	1 pt/600 ml stock
2 cloves garlic, minced	Dash soy sauce
1 small stalk celery, finely chopped	1 bay leaf
1 tin (4 oz) mild green chillies, chopped (save the juices)	½ lb/225 g mushrooms, quartered
	2–3 tablespoons fresh parsley, chopped

1 Grind pepper over both sides of the meat and press it in. Let stand for 15 minutes.
2 Heat a heavy, non-stick frying pan until moderately hot. Sear the meat on both sides. Use tongs to turn the meat.
3 Reduce heat a bit and cook for 3–4 minutes on each side. Salt lightly on both sides. Remove to a warm platter, cover loosely with foil, and keep warm.

4   Add the onion, carrot, garlic, celery, chillies, 1 teaspoon of chilli juice, oregano, tomatoes, half the stock, soy sauce, bay leaf and mushrooms to the pan. Boil, stirring and scraping the bottom of the pan until the vegetables are tender and the liquid greatly reduced. Add remaining stock. Bring to a boil and boil for 1 minute.

5   Return the meat and its accumulated meat juices to the pan and simmer, turning the beef with tongs as it cooks, for 1–2 minutes, to heat it through and cook it to your liking. To be tender the beef must remain rare, or medium rare.

6   Taste and adjust seasonings, adding a bit of salt if necessary or an extra dash of soy sauce. Discard the bay leaf. Slice the meat thinly against the grain and arrange on a warm platter. Pour the sauce over and serve at once.

Variations:

Sauté the steak (Steps 1–3) until rare or medium rare and then try one of the following:

STEAK AND MUSHROOMS

87 Calories per serving
1.1 g fat

Serve the sautéed steak simply, with Sautéed Mushrooms (see page 26). Sauté the mushrooms in the pan in which you have cooked the beef.

STEAK PIZZAIOLLA

101 Calories per serving
1 g fat

Serve the sautéed steak with Tomato Sauce (see page 151)

STEAK WITH GARLIC-WINE SAUCE

84 Calories per serving
1 g fat

When the steak has been sautéed, keep it warm. In the steak pan, boil 5 fl oz/150 ml each red wine and stock until reduced and syrupy. Add some dried crumbled thyme and tarragon if you like it. Stir in the purée of 1 head of baked garlic (see page 29). Season with salt, pepper and thyme. Slice the meat and pour the sauce over.

STEAK AND ONIONS

144 Calories per serving
1.2 g fat

The eternal classic – serve the sautéed, sliced steak with Sweet and Sour Onions (see page 26) or Browned Onions (see page 23).

STUFFED GOOSE SKIRT STEAK

Serves 4
190 Calories per serving
2 g fat

This looks like a conventional roasted joint of meat but, when sliced, reveals a beautiful pinwheel of vivid green spinach. It is also good served cold or at room temperature. Leftovers are delicious in sandwiches, with a bit of the cold sauce spread on bread.

16 fl oz/480 ml dry red wine	1 goose skirt steak (approx. 1 lb/
Juice and grated rind of ½ lemon	450 g) trimmed of any fat
2 fl oz/60 ml reduced-salt	1½ lb/675 g fresh spinach
Worcestershire sauce	Freshly ground pepper to taste
1 dried bay leaf	1 large Spanish onion, cut in half
4 cloves garlic, crushed	and sliced into thin half-moons
1 teaspoon fresh ginger, grated	

1   Preheat oven to 475° F (240° C/Gas Mark 9).
2   Combine dry red wine, lemon juice and rind, Worcestershire sauce, bay leaf, garlic and ginger in a wide, shallow non-reactive dish.
3   Butterfly the steak as follows: slit it down the long end with a very sharp knife; cut it very carefully almost all the way through until you can open it flat like a book. Or better yet, have the butcher do this for you.
4   Marinade the steak in the wine mixture while you prepare the spinach. Wash the spinach well, stem it and tear it into shreds. Put it in a non-reactive saucepan, and stir it over moderate heat, until limp, but still bright green and fresh tasting. (It will cook in the water clinging to its leaves.) Drain well. Stir in 3 tablespoons of the marinade.
5   Remove steak from the marinade. Pour the marinade into a saucepan and boil until reduced by half.
6   Open out the skirt steak. Spread the spinach over the surface to within 1 in/2.5 cm of the edges. Starting from a long edge, roll the beef like a swiss roll, into a long sausage-like shape.

Tie the roll securely crosswise in several places with kitchen string.

7   Place the beef roll on a rack in a non-reactive baking pan that can be used on top of the stove as well as in the oven. Sprinkle it with a bit of salt and a generous amount of pepper. Scatter in the onion slices. Pour in the marinade. Roast for 10 minutes. Turn it after the first 5 minutes.

8   Reduce oven temperature to 350°F (175°C/Gas Mark 4). Roast for 20 minutes more, turning it half-way through the roasting time.

9   Remove from oven. Put the beef on a platter, cover loosely with foil, and let rest for 15 minutes. Place the baking dish on the stove. Bring the pan juices to a boil. Boil until liquid is dark brown, thick and syrupy. Remove from the heat. Stir in any meat juices that have accumulated under the meat roll.

10   Remove and discard the string. Slice the meat thinly and serve, with the pan juices and the onion.

PORK MEDALLIONS ESTERHAZY

Serves 6
169 Calories per serving
1.7 g fat

My version of the classic Hungarian dish is rich and filling; a perfect choice for a winter dinner party. The original royal Hungarian version was made with beef. If you wish, serve the sauce and vegetable garnish with lean beef fillet steaks, cooked rare either under the grill or in the pan (see page 106).

---

1 pork tenderloin, trimmed of all fat   *Esterhazy sauce (recipe follows)*
Salt and freshly ground pepper   *Garnish (recipe follows)*
8 fl oz/240 ml stock

---

1   Cut the pork into ¾ in/1.9 cm slices. Sprinkle with salt and pepper.

2   Heat a heavy, non-stick frying pan until moderately hot. Sear the pork slices for 1–2 minutes on each side, until browned (do not crowd them). Pour in the stock, simmer, turning frequently, for approximately 5 minutes, until cooked through and tender. Transfer to a plate, cover loosely and keep warm.

3   Boil the stock for a few seconds, scraping the bottom of the pan with a wooden spatula. When the stock is thick and syrupy,

reduce the heat and add the pork slices back to the pan. With tongs, turn a few times.

4   Arrange the pork on a warm platter. Stir the syrupy stock into the Esterhazy sauce. Pour some sauce over the pork. Top with the drained, hot vegetable garnish. Serve at once. Pass the rest of the sauce at the table.

ESTERHAZY SAUCE

67 Calories for the entire sauce recipe
0.5 g fat

This is one of the most delicious sauces I know. Its richness is amazing, yet it contains virtually no fat. It may be made ahead of time and stored in the refrigerator. Bring to room temperature before proceeding with the recipe.

---

1 large onion, chopped
2 small carrots, peeled and chopped
2 small parsnips, peeled and chopped
1 pt/600 ml stock
1 dried bay leaf

Salt and freshly ground pepper to taste
Grated zest of 1 lemon
Juice of ½ a lemon
1 tablespoon Dijon mustard
4 fl oz/120 ml quark mixed with 1½ fl oz/45 ml skimmed milk

---

1   Combine the vegetables with 4 fl oz/120 ml stock in a heavy frying pan. Cover and simmer briskly for 4–5 minutes. Uncover and simmer until the vegetables are almost tender and the liquid just about gone.
2   Add remaining stock, bay leaf, salt, pepper, lemon zest and lemon juice. Let simmer gently, uncovered, until the vegetables are very tender. Discard bay leaf. Cool slightly. Purée the mixture in a liquidizer with the mustard and the quark. Pour it into a saucepan.
3   Simmer gently for approximately 5 minutes. Taste and adjust seasonings. Remove from heat. Cover with a piece of cling film directly over the surface of the sauce and set aside until needed.

GARNISH

This is good enough to serve as a vegetable accompaniment to other dishes on occasion, or use to top fish fillets *en papillote* (see page 80).

1 parsnip	*8 fl oz/240 ml stock*
1 carrot	*Salt and freshly ground pepper to*
1 stalk celery	*taste*

1   Scrape the vegetables and cut them into julienne. Combine with the stock and simmer briskly, stirring constantly, until tender, and the stock is thickened and reduced. Season to taste.
2   Set aside until needed.

Poultry

'There is no way of preparing a chicken
which I don't like'

Marcella Hazan – *Marcella's Kitchen*, 1987

C hicken is famous for being low fat and good for you, but it needs some help before it can live up to its reputation. Be ruthless with the chicken that you take home from the store. Pull off all the lumps of fat. (There will be several and they will be large.) Denude the bird of its fatty skin – all of it. Only then is the chicken ready for Slim Cuisine. The white meat is leaner than the dark, and each requires different handling.

Chicken Breasts

Skinless, boneless chicken breasts are perfect for a quick, elegant meal. When properly cooked, they have a remarkably creamy and delicate texture. If they are overcooked, however, they become stringy and dry. Many quality butchers and supermarkets carry chicken breasts from free-range birds that have been skinned, boned and split. When you get them home, meticulously trim away any traces of fat, gristle and skin. Under each chicken breast is a loose, narrow flap of flesh. Pull it off and save it for stir-fries, or chicken salad. The trimmed deflapped chicken breast is called the 'supreme' or the 'cutlet'. A 3½ oz/100 g chicken cutlet contains approximately 104 Calories and negligible fat. It is an excellent source of protein. It can be quickly pan-sautéed in a heavy non-stick frying pan and served with a delicate sauce. Sauté the chicken until it is just done, so that it is tender and plumply juicy.

PAN-SAUTÉED CHICKEN BREASTS

Heat a heavy, non-stick frying pan until moderately hot. Season the chicken with salt and pepper. Cook for 3 minutes on the skinned side, then carefully turn and cook on the second side, for approximately 3 minutes or until *just* cooked through (it will feel firm but a little springy when touched with your finger).

Chicken breasts prepared in this manner may be used with a variety of sauces, either hot or cold. Consider the following:

Yellow Pepper Sauce	(page 119)
Red Pepper Sauce	(page 146)
Beet Purée	(page 164)
Hungarian Green Sauce	(page 144)
Esterhazy Sauce	(page 111)
Tomato Sauce	(page 151)
Remoulade Sauce	(page 58)
Pesto	(page 145)

Or top the breasts with Sautéed Mushrooms (page 26) and shredded Mozzarella cheese. Grill for 1–2 minutes until the cheese is melted and bubbly.

Chicken Legs and Thighs

Unlike the breasts, the dark meat of chicken takes beautifully to slow, gentle braising. When cooked with flavoursome ingredients, the meat becomes succulent and comforting; perfect cold-weather fare. Before cooking the legs and thighs, remove and discard all skin and fat. For many braised dishes, consider cooking the dish the day before serving. Store it in the refrigerator. The next day, any fat in the sauce will have congealed. Spoon it out and discard it. Then reheat the casserole and serve. And remember that the meat from free-range birds is the most delicious.

CHICKEN-BERRY SALAD

Serves 6
176 Calories per serving
0.9 g fat

This is the most elegant of chicken salads. Serve it as a main dish at a light supper or a special luncheon. With its berries, creamy-textured chicken breast and light dressing, this salad is the essence of summer. Shredded poached chicken may be substituted for the chicken cutlets, or use smoked chicken.

---

6 chicken cutlets (see page 114)
1 lb/450 g mixed fresh berries (use blueberries, blackberries, strawberries, raspberries, whatever you can find)
½ lb/225 g seedless grapes

8 oz/224 g drained low-fat fromage blanc
Juice of ½ small lemon
½ teaspoon mild honey
2 tablespoons buttermilk
Salt and freshly ground pepper to taste
Fresh mint leaves

---

1 Cook the chicken according to the pan-sauté method (see page 114).

2 Slice each chicken cutlet into crosswise wide slices on the diagonal. Overlap them on a pretty platter. Surround the chicken with the mixed berries and grapes.

3 Combine remaining ingredients except mint leaves. Pour a bit of dressing in a stripe down the centre of the chicken slices. Garnish with mint leaves. Serve the rest of the dressing separately.

MOULDED CHICKEN SALAD

Serves 10
85 Calories per serving
0.4 g fat
(traditional chicken salad: 234 Calories per serving, 18 g fat)

This is lovely as a luncheon dish or as a first course for a special dinner party. It makes a good sandwich filling too. Be sure that you season it well. It should not be bland.

Juice of 1 lemon	*1 large stalk celery, finely minced*
6 tablespoons chopped chives	*2 poached chickens (use the poached*
8 tablespoons chopped fresh dill	*chicken left from making stock or*
8 tablespoons chopped fresh parsley	*see recipe for quick poached*
⅕ pt/120 ml yoghurt cream cheese	*chicken, page 128)*
(see recipe)	*Salt and freshly ground pepper to*
Buttermilk	*taste*
Cayenne pepper	*Watercress*

1   Combine lemon juice, herbs, yoghurt cheese, 5 tablespoons buttermilk, cayenne pepper and celery in a large bowl.
2   Pull the chicken from the bones in chunks and shred it finely with your fingers. As you shred each chunk, stir it into the bowl. Discard every bit of fat, skin and gristle.
3   Stir in more buttermilk until the texture is creamy but not too loose. Season to taste with salt and freshly ground pepper and more cayenne if desired. The flavour should be very lively.
4   Tightly pack the mixture into a 1¼ pt/750 ml mould (heart-shaped is nice). Cover and refrigerate overnight. The mixture will taste quite yoghurty at first but it will mellow overnight until it tastes as if it were made with a lemony mayonnaise.
5   At serving time, loosen the mousse all round with a thin-bladed knife. Unmould onto a pretty serving plate. Garnish with watercress and serve.

CURRIED CHICKEN SALAD

Serves 10
133 Calories per serving
0.4 g fat

This is an elegant, spicy version of the moulded chicken salad. It's a show-stopping buffet dish.

7 shallots, peeled and chopped
8 oz/224 g sultanas
4 fl oz/120 ml chicken stock
4 fl oz/120 ml raspberry vinegar
2 teaspoons minced fresh ginger
4 cloves garlic, minced
1 teaspoon turmeric
2 teaspoons each: ground cumin,
   ground coriander, ground
   cinnamon
¼ teaspoon ground cloves

½ teaspoon ground chillies
½ teaspoon ground allspice
⅕ pt/120 ml yoghurt cream cheese
Buttermilk
8 tablespoons chopped fresh parsley
1 large stalk celery, finely minced
2 poached chickens
Salt, freshly ground pepper and
   cayenne pepper to taste
Fresh coriander

1   Spread the shallot pieces in a heavy, non-stick frying pan. Add *no* liquid or fat. Heat the frying pan gently. Cook at moderate heat, without stirring, for 7–10 minutes, until the shallots are sizzling, speckled with dark amber, and beginning to stick to the pan.

2   Stir in the sultanas, stock, and raspberry vinegar and let it bubble up, stirring up the browned deposits in the pan with a wooden spoon as it bubbles. Stir in the ginger, garlic and spices. Turn the heat down a bit and simmer, stirring frequently, until the mixture is very thick (not at all soupy), and the shallots and spices are 'frying' in their own juices. Don't rush this step, it is essential that the spices should not have a raw harsh taste. Taste. Cook very gently for a few more minutes if necessary. Cool.

3   Combine the cooled mixture with the yoghurt, 5 tablespoons of buttermilk, parsley and celery in a large bowl.

4   Pull the chicken from the bones in chunks and shred each chunk into the bowl. Discard every bit of fat, skin and gristle.

5   Stir in more buttermilk until the texture is creamy but not too loose. Season with salt, freshly ground pepper and cayenne if you want it very spicy. Tightly pack the mixture into a mould as described in the previous recipe. Refrigerate overnight. At serving time, unmould onto a pretty plate and garnish with fresh coriander.

OVEN-'FRIED' CHICKEN WITH CREAMY MINT DIPPING SAUCE

Makes 8 pieces of chicken
130 Calories per 'fried' chicken leg
2.4 g fat
(traditional fried chicken: 232 Calories per piece, 7.3 g fat)

Oven-'frying' produces juicy, crispy-crusted chicken that is prepared without a speck of oil or fat. The dipping sauce is Indian-inspired.

⅗ pt/360 ml plain yoghurt	4 chicken thighs, skinned
⅖ pt/240 ml breadcrumbs	4 chicken legs, skinned
Salt and freshly ground pepper to taste	Dipping sauce (recipe follows)

1 Preheat oven to 400° F (200° C/Gas Mark 6).
2 Pour the yoghurt into a wide, shallow bowl and set it on your work surface.
3 Season the breadcrumbs with salt and pepper. Spread crumbs out on a platter and place next to the yoghurt.
4 Place a wire rack over a baking sheet and set aside.
5 Dry the chicken pieces. Dip each piece into the yoghurt until thoroughly coated on both sides. Then roll each piece in the crumbs, pressing the piece in so that the crumbs adhere. Each piece should be evenly coated.
6 Place the chicken on the wire rack. Bake for 40–45 minutes, or until just done.
7 To serve, place a piece of chicken on each of four small plates. Pour some sauce in a crescent on the bottom edge of each plate, around the chicken but not on it. Put the remaining pieces of chicken on a platter and pass the remaining sauce in a clear jug.

Note: If you don't use dairy produce with meat, dip the chicken into egg white instead of yoghurt and choose a vegetable purée sauce (see index) instead of the following one.

DIPPING SAUCE

182 Calories entire recipe
0.6 g fat

⅗ pt/360 ml plain low-fat yoghurt	Salt to taste
½ small onion, coarsely chopped	6 tablespoons fresh mint leaves
1 thin slice ginger root, peeled and chopped	2 tablespoons fresh coriander (Chinese parsley) leaves
1 teaspoon chopped fresh chillies (or more to taste)	2 tablespoons fresh parsley leaves

Place all the ingredients in a blender or food processor. Flick the motor on and off until a thin, flecked green sauce is achieved. Serve at once.

CHICKEN WITH YELLOW PEPPER SAUCE

Makes 4 pieces
124 Calories per piece
0.7 g fat

The rich, buttery yellow pepper sauce complements the juicy chicken cutlet very well. You will find the sauce useful in many other ways as well.

---

4 fl oz/120 ml dry white wine or
   dry vermouth
3 fl oz/90 ml tarragon wine vinegar
2 tablespoons minced shallots
½ teaspoon dried tarragon,
   crumbled

1 tablespoon chopped fresh parsley
6 yellow peppers, coarsely diced
½ pt/300 ml stock
Pinch of cayenne pepper
Salt and freshly ground pepper
4 chicken cutlets (see page 114)

---

1   Combine the first five ingredients in a small saucepan. Bring to the boil, reduce heat and simmer briskly until almost all the liquid has evaporated. Set aside.
2   Combine the peppers and stock in a deep, heavy frying pan. Bring to a boil. Cover, reduce heat and simmer for 20–30 minutes, until tender. Cool.
3   Purée the peppers in a liquidizer or food processor. Strain through a sieve or strainer, rubbing it through with a rubber spatula or a wooden spoon. The skins will be left behind. Discard them.
4   Put the purée in a saucepan. Simmer for a few minutes until it is thick enough to coat the back of a spoon. Stir in the tarragon infusion and season to taste with salt and pepper. This sauce may be prepared several days ahead and stored in the refrigerator until needed. Warm it while the chicken is cooking.
5   Heat a heavy, non-stick frying pan until moderately hot. Season the chicken with salt and pepper. Cook for 3 minutes on the skinned side, then carefully turn and cook on the second side for approximately 3 minutes or until *just* cooked through. (It will feel firm but a little springy when touched with your finger.) Place the chicken on a plate and cover loosely.

6   Stir any juices that have accumulated under the chicken into the hot yellow pepper sauce. Ladle a generous amount of the sauce onto warm dinner plates. Slice each chicken cutlet crosswise into ½ in/1.3 cm slices. Overlap the slices from each cutlet on the puddle of sauce. Serve at once.

CHICKEN WITH RASPBERRIES

Makes 4 pieces
102 Calories per piece
0.4 g fat

This is one of the most exciting chicken breast recipes I know. The garlic cloves are cooked and served like a vegetable. Use fresh, firm, unblemished bulbs. The manner of cooking ensures that they become tender and mild – not the slightest bit overpowering or 'garlicky'. If the thought of raspberries with garlic is just too shocking, omit the raspberry garnish (but not the raspberry juice – it is essential to the goodness of the sauce). Although you have to thaw a package of frozen raspberries to get the little bit of juice needed, you can make a batch of Raspberry Sauce (see page 209) with the thawed berries for use in a dessert, later in the week.

---

16 large garlic cloves	*4 chicken cutlets (see page 114)*
1 teaspoon sugar	*Salt and freshly ground pepper to*
3½ tablespoons raspberry vinegar	*taste*
4 fl oz/120 ml water	*Raspberry juice and a few*
4 fl oz/120 ml chicken stock	*raspberries for garnish*

Note: Use thawed frozen raspberries for the garnish. Some of the juice will be used in Step 4 to augment the sauce.

1   Combine garlic, sugar, ½ tablespoon vinegar and ½ tablespoon water in a small saucepan. Bring to a boil. Reduce heat and simmer, uncovered, for about 3 minutes, until sugar dissolves. Increase the heat to a rapid simmer, cover, and let cook until the garlic is tender, and caramelized, and the liquid is just about gone, about 10 minutes.

2   Add the stock and the remaining vinegar and boil, uncovered, for another minute. Set aside.

3   Heat a heavy, non-stick frying pan until moderately hot. Season the chicken with salt and pepper. Cook for 3 minutes on the skinned side, then carefully turn and cook on the second side for approximately 3 minutes or until *just* cooked

through. (The pieces will feel firm but a little springy when touched with your finger.) Place the chicken on a plate and cover loosely.

4   Add the sauce and the garlic to the frying pan. Bring to a boil, stirring and scraping with a wooden spoon as you do so. Add 1–2 tablespoons of juice from the thawed raspberries. After about a minute the sauce will be thick and syrupy. Remove from the heat. Taste and season with a tiny bit of salt and some pepper.

5   Pour any juices that have accumulated under the chicken into the sauce. Add the chicken and turn it to coat with the sauce. Arrange the chicken on a serving plate. Pour the sauce and the garlic over and around it. Place a few berries on each plate for garnish. Serve at once.

CHICKEN CURRY

Serves 6
148 Calories per serving
0.6 g fat

This is an exquisite dish, excellent served warm, tepid or cool. It does not reheat well. The only tricky thing about the recipe is the timing. You want to catch the chicken at the exact moment of doneness, when it is creamy, tender and perfect.

6 skinless, boneless chicken breasts	½ bay leaf, finely crumbled
Juice of 1 large lemon	2 cloves garlic, minced
Salt to taste	2 medium onions, cut into eighths
1 teaspoon each: ground turmeric, ground cumin, ground coriander	10 fl oz/300 ml stock
	4 fl oz/120 ml stock
½ teaspoon each: caster sugar, ground chillies, ground cinnamon	2 tablespoons tomato paste
	1 oz/28 g raisins
	3 tablespoons plain low-fat yoghurt, at room temperature

1   Cut the chicken breasts crosswise into strips that are approximately 1 in/2.5 cm wide. Each breast will yield about 5 strips. Put the strips in a bowl, squeeze the lemon juice over them, sprinkle with a bit of salt, and toss with two spoons to combine. Set aside.

2   Measure all the spices and herbs into a small bowl. Add the minced garlic.

3   Separate the segments of the onion pieces and spread them in a heavy, non-stick, frying pan. Add *no* liquid or fat. Heat the

frying pan gently. Cook at moderate heat, without stirring, for 7–10 minutes, until the onions are sizzling, speckled with dark amber, and beginning to stick to the pan.

4   Stir in 10 fl oz/300 ml stock and let it bubble up, stirring up the browned deposits in the pan with a wooden spoon as it bubbles. Stir in the spices and garlic. Turn the heat down a bit and simmer, stirring frequently, until the mixture is very thick (not at all soupy), and the onions and spices are 'frying' in their own juices. Don't rush this step, as it is essential that the spices should not have a raw harsh taste. Taste. Cook very gently for a few more minutes if necessary.

5   Toss the chicken into the spicy onions in the frying pan. Stir and turn the chicken over low heat for 1 minute until everything is well combined. Stir in 4 fl oz/120 ml of stock and the tomato paste and raisins. Spread the mixture out evenly in the pan. Cover and cook over *lowest* heat for 4 minutes more.

6   Uncover. Add 2 tablespoons yoghurt. Stir over *low* heat for a few moments, until everything is amalgamated. Stir in the last tablespoon of yoghurt and cook, stirring, for a moment or two more. Check the chicken for doneness. It should feel firm and springy, not soft and mushy. If you wish, cut into several pieces. You may even cut each strip in half. Each piece should be pearly white in the centre. Try to catch them when they are *just* done, at the moment they are turning from blush pink to creamy white, A minute or two of overcooking turns them tough and stringy. If they are not done yet, clap on the cover, turn off the heat and let them sit for a minute or two more. Stir everything up once more and serve warm or at room temperature.

Note: Although the dish does *not* reheat well from the refrigerator, it does beautifully from the freezer. Freeze individual portions of this if you wish. To reheat, microwave, still frozen, for 4 minutes on high. It will be as perfect as if it were freshly prepared.

CHICKEN IN ONION-TOMATO GRAVY

Makes 12 pieces
90 Calories per piece
1.6 g fat

This homely chicken dish has an Indian accent. It is best made in advance so that the flavours mellow and the congealed fat can be removed the next day.

4 large onions	1 pinch ground cloves
15 fl oz/450 ml stock	8 cardamom pods, lightly crushed
1 tablespoon minced fresh peeled ginger	1 bay leaf, broken in half
4 cloves garlic, minced	2 cinnamon sticks, broken in halves
1 teaspoon ground cumin	2 tins (14 oz/392 g each) chopped tomatoes
1 teaspoon ground coriander	6 chicken legs, skinned
½ teaspoon cayenne pepper (to taste)	6 chicken thighs, skinned
	Salt and pepper to taste

1   Separate the segments of the onion pieces and spread them in a heavy, non-stick, frying pan. Add *no* liquid or fat. Heat the frying pan gently. Cook at moderate heat, without stirring, for 7–10 minutes, until the onions are sizzling, speckled with dark amber, and beginning to stick to the pan.

2   Stir in 10 fl oz/300 ml of stock and let it bubble up, stirring up the browned deposits in the pan with a wooden spoon as it bubbles. Stir in the ginger, garlic and spices. Turn the heat down a bit and simmer, stirring frequently, until the mixture is very thick (not at all soupy), and the onions and spices are 'frying' in their own juices. Don't rush this step – it is essential that the spices should not have a raw harsh taste. Taste. Cook very gently for a few more minutes if necessary.

3   Stir the tomatoes into the onions. Set the pan aside.

4   Place the chicken thighs, skinned side down, in a non-stick frying pan. Heat gently until the chicken is sizzling. Do not add fat or oil! Brown the chicken thighs lightly on the skinned side, season with salt and pepper, turn and brown lightly on the other side. Blot them with paper towels, then place them, skinned side down, in one layer, on the tomato mixture. Repeat with the chicken legs. Place them between and over the thighs. Blot the pan with paper towels in order to mop up the rendered fat.

5   Pour the remaining stock into the frying pan and boil rapidly, until it is reduced by more than half. Stir and scrape up the browned bits on the bottom of the frying pan as it boils. Pour the stock over the chicken.

6   Bring the tomato-chicken mixture to a boil. Reduce heat, cover, and simmer for 20 minutes.

7   At the end of 20 minutes, turn and rearrange the chicken pieces in the pan. Cover and simmer until the chicken is done, 20–30 minutes more.

8   Remove the chicken to a casserole or a platter. Cover loosely with foil so that it does not dry out. Tip the pan and skim as much fat as possible from the sauce. Boil the sauce for a few

minutes, until it is thick and pulpy. Recombine the chicken and sauce, cover, cool somewhat, and refrigerate.

9   The next day, scrape out the congealed fat and discard it. Reheat the chicken and sauce gently.

BRAISED HONEY-MUSTARD CHICKEN

Makes 12 pieces
78 Calories per piece
1.6 g fat

Serve this with rice to soak up the mustardy juices.

1½ tablespoons honey	6 chicken legs, skinned
Juice of ½ a lemon	6 chicken thighs, skinned
2 cloves garlic, minced	Salt and freshly ground pepper to
½ teaspoon soy sauce	taste
1–2 pinches cayenne pepper	1 medium onion, coarsely chopped
2 tablespoons Dijon mustard	

1   Preheat oven to 325° F (170°C/Gas Mark 3).
2   In a small bowl, stir together the honey, lemon, garlic, soy sauce, cayenne pepper and mustard.
3   Season the chicken with salt and pepper. Put the chicken and onions in a casserole. Pour and scrape the mustard mixture over the chicken. Mix together very well so that the chicken and onions are coated with the sauce. Cover the baking dish with foil so that no steam can escape.
4   Bake for 1½ hours.

CHICKEN BRAISED WITH GARLIC

Makes 12 pieces
78 Calories per piece
1.5 g fat
(traditional chicken braised with garlic: 166 Calories per piece, 2.8 g fat)

This is my low-fat version of a famous French classic. *Everyone* loves this dish, even confirmed garlic-haters. Slow, gentle cooking renders the usually pungent bulb sweet, mild and mysterious.

40 *cloves garlic (see note)*
6 *chicken legs, skinned*
6 *chicken thighs, skinned*
2 *medium onions, coarsely chopped*
2 *sticks celery, thinly sliced (save*
  the leaves)
¼ *pt/150 ml chopped fresh parsley*
1 *teaspoon dried tarragon,*
  crumbled

½ *teaspoon allspice*
¼ *teaspoon cinnamon*
Pinch cayenne pepper
Salt and freshly ground pepper to
  taste
2 *fl oz/60 ml cognac*
3 *fl oz/90 ml dry white vermouth*

1   Preheat oven to 325° F (170° C/Gas Mark 3).
2   Place all ingredients in a deep, heavy pot that can be covered. Combine everything very well with your hands. Seal the pot very tightly with foil. Place the pot cover over the foil. The pot must be very well sealed so that no juices or steam can escape.
3   Bake for 1½ hours. Do not open the pot during this time.
4   Serve piping hot, with good crusty bread for mopping up the garlic and the juices. Open the pot at the table so that the diners get a blast of the wonderful fragrance that emerges as you open it.

Note: The garlic must be fresh and unblemished with no shrivelled cloves or green sprouts. If you wish, peel the garlic first, by parboiling the cloves for 3 minutes in water to cover, then slipping off the skins. If you are in a rush, however, throw in the garlic unpeeled. As it cooks, it will become a purée within its skin. Encourage diners to squeeze the purée out of the skin with their forks and spread it on bread. Garlic haters can ignore it completely, although they will be missing something marvellous if they do. Have a few empty plates on the table to receive the discarded garlic husks and the gnawed chicken bones. Both this and the preceding Honey-Mustard Chicken should be made a day ahead of time and reheated – the flavour will improve. Cook the dish for only 1¼ hours on the first day, cool and refrigerate. On the next day, scrape off the congealed fat, then reheat gently, covered, in the oven.

Variations:
Use the procedure in the preceding 2 recipes but try these combinations of ingredients:

Chicken Cacciatore: tomatoes, mushrooms, wine
Oreganato: lemon juice, oregano, onions, wine, garlic
Indian-Style: cardamom, cumin, coriander, cayenne, lemon juice
          and rind, onion, garlic, fresh coriander

American Barbecued: tomato purée, browned onions, cider vinegar, chillies, dash Worcestershire sauce, 1–2 pinches brown sugar

CHICKEN VINDALOO

Makes 8 pieces
69 Calories per piece
1.5 g fat
(traditional chicken vindaloo: 307 Calories per piece, 12 g fat)

Indian vindaloos are sour and spicy, and beautifully pungent. Freeze leftovers and then microwave. I find that if refrigerated and then reheated on top of the cooker, the leftovers tend to dry out. The same holds true for the next recipe, Chicken Bhuna.

2–3 tiny chilli peppers, thickly sliced
1 medium onion, cut into chunks
2 cloves garlic, lightly crushed
1 piece (2 in/5 cm long) fresh ginger, peeled and cut into chunks

1 teaspoon whole cumin seeds
1 teaspoon whole coriander seeds
1 teaspoon turmeric
1 teaspoon whole mustard seeds
2 tablespoon white vinegar
8 chicken legs, skin and fat removed
Salt to taste

---

1   Combine all ingredients except chicken and salt in the liquidizer. Purée the mixture, stopping to scrape down the sides of the container with a rubber spatula.
2   Slash each chicken leg in 2–3 places with a sharp knife. Toss the chicken and spice paste together. Allow to marinate for at least 1 hour.
3   Gently heat a heavy, non-stick frying pan that can hold the pieces of chicken in one layer. When moderately hot, put in the chicken pieces and spice paste. Cook gently for 1–2 minutes, turning the chicken with tongs, until it has just lost its raw look. Do not brown it.
4   Turn the heat to the lowest point. Cover the pan tightly and cook for about 1 hour, or until the chicken is very tender. Turn the chicken every 15 minutes or so.

CHICKEN BHUNA

Makes 8 pieces
79 Calories per piece
1.9 g fat
(traditional chicken bhuna: 323 Calories per piece, 12 g fat)

Eat this vibrant Indian dish at once, it does not hold well. Freeze any leftovers (although there probably won't be any) and microwave.

---

1 medium onion, chopped	1 teaspoon ground cumin
10 fl oz/300 ml stock	1 teaspoon chilli powder
2 cloves garlic, minced	Pinch cloves
1 teaspoon chopped fresh peeled ginger	½ bay leaf, broken in half
	1 tablespoon grated coconut
1 teaspoon turmeric	2–3 tablespoons tomato paste
½ teaspoon ground cinnamon	8 chicken thighs, skinned
½ teaspoon grated nutmeg	Chopped fresh coriander
½ teaspoon ground allspice	

---

1   Spread the onions in a heavy, non-stick, frying pan. Add *no* liquid or fat. Heat the frying pan gently. Cook at moderate heat, without stirring, for 7–10 minutes, until the onions are sizzling, speckled with dark amber, and beginning to stick to the pan.

2   Stir in 10 fl oz/300 ml of stock and let it bubble up, stirring up the browned deposits in the pan with a wooden spoon as it bubbles. Stir in the ginger, garlic and spices. Turn the heat down a bit and simmer, stirring frequently, until the mixture is very thick (not at all soupy), and the onions and spices are 'frying' in their own juices. Don't rush this step, it is essential that the spices should not have a raw harsh taste. Taste. Cook very gently for a few more minutes if necessary.

3   Stir in the coconut and tomato paste. Add the chicken and stir it around to coat it thoroughly with the spice mixture.

4   Cover and cook over the lowest possible heat for about 1 hour, until the chicken is very tender. Turn the pieces occasionally. Serve garnished with coriander.

CHICKEN TARRAGON PIE

Serves 6
236 Calories per serving
6 g fat

Here is a satisfying and interesting main course that uses both the tender chicken meat left over from making stock, and the Slim Cuisine onion-herb infusion. It is a sort of souffléd, savoury bread pudding. Serve with a salad of dark, leafy greens sprinkled with an interesting vinegar – balsamic, sherry or raspberry. The more interesting the vinegar, the less you will miss the olive oil. Because it contains high-fat eggs, make this pie only occasionally. If you do not have a poached chicken on hand, use the quick poached chicken recipe, (see below) or buy a ready-cooked chicken from the supermarket. The recipe also works beautifully with a smoked chicken. Be sure to remove all skin and fat before using it.

---

6 oz/168 g stale bread torn into
   chunks
1 recipe onion-herb infusion (use
   tarragon as the herb, see page
   24)
1 small poached or smoked chicken,
   shredded
2 oz/56 g part-skim Mozzarella,
   shredded

2 tablespoons grated Parmesan
   cheese
3 tablespoons chopped fresh parsley
3 eggs
4 fl oz/120 ml buttermilk
12 fl oz/360 ml skimmed milk
Salt, freshly ground pepper and
   cayenne pepper to taste

---

1   Preheat the oven to 350° F (180° C/Gas Mark 4).
2   In a bowl, toss together the bread, the infusion, the chicken, the cheeses and the parsley. Spread this mixture in a 9 × 13 in (23 × 33 cm) shallow glass or ceramic baking dish.
3   Beat the eggs with the buttermilk. Gradually beat in the skimmed milk. Season with salt and peppers to taste. You will need very little salt because the infusion, the Parmesan and the peppers give plenty of flavour. Pour this mixture over the bread mixture. With a broad spatula or pancake turner, press the bread down into the liquid.
4   Bake for 40–45 minutes until puffed and set. A knife inserted near the centre should come out clean.

POACHED CHICKEN

If you do not need to make stock and you want to poach a chicken in a hurry, use this nifty technique taught to me by a Chinese friend.

---

1 chicken (2½ lb/1,125 g)
Boiling water (10 pts/4,730 ml)

A ragout of wild and cultivated mushrooms (page 167)
appetizingly heaped into crunchy potato cases (page 172).
Potato gratin (page 173): meltingly tender potato
slices in a creamy sauce under a crusty top.

1   Bring the water to a boil in a deep pot.
2   Pull all excess fat from the chicken and wash well, inside and out, in cold water. Submerge the chicken in the boiling water. When the water returns to a full boil, cover and boil hard for 12 minutes (5 minutes per lb/450 g).
3   Remove the pot from the heat and let the chicken cool in the pot. (Do not leave it to cool at room temperature for more than 2 hours. It can, however, be refrigerated, pot, cooking liquid, and all, overnight.)
4   Remove it from the liquid. (It will still be quite warm so be careful.) Remove the skin. Pull the meat off the bones in large pieces. Discard all tendons and gristle. Tear the meat into chunks or shred it. Refrigerate in a shallow dish, moistened with a bit of stock and well covered with cling film until needed. Needless to say, this chicken is lovely in chicken salad. Or try it in Chilaquiles.

CHILAQUILES

Serves 6
209 Calories per serving
5 g fat

This is an exciting, unusual and splendid recipe; a low-fat version of authentic Mexican home cooking. There are many versions, but they always involve layers of corn tortilla pieces and piquant sauce. Sometimes meat or, as here, chicken is layered in too. The original versions are swimming in fat. I have used the recipe successfully with a smoked chicken, and if you are in a hurry you might want to use a ready-cooked chicken from the supermarket. Just be sure that you remove all skin and fat before using it. Corn tortillas (Old El Paso brand) are available in tins in many supermarkets and delicatessens. Reduce the amount of chilli peppers if you don't like spicy food.

Salad delights: clockwise from top right:
greens with creamy herbed dressing (page 183); ripe tomatoes
and Mozzarella cheese with shredded basil (page 185);
fennel-pepper salad with mushrooms and capers (page 187).

1 pt/600 ml chicken stock
1 large onion, chopped
1 medium fresh chilli pepper, seeded
  and coarsely diced
2 tiny fresh chilli peppers, diced
4 jalapeños tinned in vinegar,
  drained and coarsely diced
2 tins (1 lb/450 g each) chopped
  tomatoes
2 cloves garlic
Salt to taste

5 corn tortillas, baked in a 400° F
  (200° C/Gas Mark 7) oven for
  3–4 minutes, broken into pieces
  (see page 198)
Meat from 1 (2–2½ lb/1,125 g)
  poached chicken (see chicken
  stock recipe or quick poached
  chicken recipe)
6 oz/168 g part-skim Mozzarella
  cheese, shredded

1   In a heavy non-reactive frying pan, combine the onion in 4 fl·
    oz/120 ml stock, cover and bring to a boil. Reduce heat and
    simmer for 5 minutes. Uncover, raise heat and simmer very
    briskly until almost all liquid has boiled away. Reduce heat
    and simmer gently until the liquid is gone and the onions are
    beginning to stick. Stir until they begin to toast and brown.
    Pour in a splash of stock and boil, stirring and scraping the
    browned bits on the bottom of the pan. Remove from the heat.
2   Place the chillies, jalapeños, tomatoes and garlic in the liquid-
    izer. Blend to a smooth purée. Pour into the frying pan with
    the onions. Cook over low heat, stirring for a few minutes.
3   Add the remaining stock, and salt to taste, to the tomato
    mixture. Simmer, uncovered, for 35–45 minutes, until thick
    and pungent. At this point the sauce is almost hot enough to
    melt the frying pan. When it is mixed with the remaining
    ingredients, however, its piquancy will be somewhat diluted.
4   Preheat the oven to 350° F (180° C/Gas Mark 4).
5   Layer ⅓ of the tortilla pieces, ⅓ of the sauce, ⅓ of the
    shredded chicken, and ⅓ of the cheese in a shallow non-
    reactive gratin dish or baking dish. Layer in the second ⅓ of
    tortilla pieces, sauce, chicken and cheese. Layer on the re-
    maining tortilla pieces, the chicken, the cheese and the sauce.
6   Bake, uncovered, for 35 minutes until bubbly. Serve at once.

BREAST OF DUCKLING À L'ORANGE

Serves 4
151 Calories per serving
5 g fat

For duck lovers, this is as elegant and ducky as can be, without the quantities of fat usually found in duck preparations. Duck breast fillets are available all the year round in selected supermarkets throughout the UK. They are traditionally cooked medium rare (pink). Cooked this way, duck breast meat bears an uncanny resemblance to the finest beef steak.

---

4 duckling breast fillets
¼ teaspoon ground cumin
¼ teaspoon ground ginger
Freshly ground pepper
Salt to taste

4 fl oz/120 ml fresh orange juice
4 fl oz/120 ml chicken or duck stock
2 fl oz/60 ml dry red wine
½ teaspoon red wine vinegar

---

1   Work your fingers between the duckling flesh and the skin. Gently and steadily pull the skin from each breast fillet. It should strip right off. Use a sharp knife to help loosen it, should you hit a stubborn spot. Discard the skin and trim off and discard any fat and gristle on the fillets.

2   Combine the cumin and ginger. Sprinkle some of the spice mixture onto both sides of the duck breast fillets and rub it in. Sprinkle both sides of each fillet generously with freshly ground pepper and press it in. Set the fillets aside for 15 minutes.

3   Heat a heavy, non-stick frying pan until quite hot. It should be of a size to hold the fillets without letting them touch one another. When hot, salt the fillets lightly, and place them, skinned side up, in the pan. Cook for 3–4 minutes on each side, until medium rare (pink within). Use tongs to turn them. Test for the proper degree of doneness by poking them with your finger. If they feel mushy, they are very rare. If they feel firm, but springy, they are medium rare. If they feel quite firm with no springiness, they are well done and, in my opinion, overcooked.

4   Remove the fillets and blot gently with paper towels to remove any rendered fat. Put them on a warm platter, cover loosely with foil and set aside in a warm place. An oven set at its lowest point is perfect.

5   Gently blot the frying pan with paper towels, to remove any fat. Pour orange juice, stock, wine and wine vinegar into the

pan. It will boil up furiously. Let it boil, stirring and scraping up the browned bits in the pan with a wooden spoon. When thickened and syrupy, remove from the heat. Stir in any juices that have accumulated under the fillets.

6   Slice each fillet into thin slices, on the diagonal, crosswise. Overlap them on warm plates. Pour the sauce over them. Serve at once.

Vegetarian

'An attachment à la Plato for a
bashful young potato or a not too
French French Bean'

W. S. Gilbert – *Patience* 1881

A meal does not always have to be focused on meat, poultry or fish. Vegetables can easily be the star of a meal. There are vegetable recipes in other sections of the book as well that can be served as vegetarian main courses. Check the pasta and potato sections in particular.

VEGETARIAN FONDUE

This is one of my favourite meals, for guests as well as just family. It's colourful, fun and unusual. Add protein by serving a starter that contains quark, yoghurt cheese, fromage blanc, fish etc., (see the Starter chapter for ideas), or end with one of the buttermilk-based icecreams in the Dessert chapter. Choose your vegetables according to the season, and cook them carefully so that they are just done – flabby, mushy vegetables are unlovely things. Steaming is the best way to achieve perfection, both from a nutritional and culinary standpoint.

A selection of fresh vegetables, each steamed until just done. Consider:

Cauliflower	*(in florets)*
New potatoes	*(unpeeled)*
Broccoli	*(in florets)*
Small turnips	*(quartered)*
French beans	
Mangetout	
Asparagus	*(peeled and trimmed)*
Courgettes	*(cut into sticks)*
Sautéed whole button mushrooms	*(see page 26)*

A selection of hot and cold sauces. Consider:

Red Pepper Sauce	*Remoulade Sauce*
Yellow Pepper Sauce	*Tomato Sauce*
Beetroot Purée	*Pesto*
Hungarian Green Sauce	

If you decide you'd like to add meat, choose a meatball recipe (see page 89) and offer some as part of the selection. Arrange everything with colour, texture and shape in mind and, if you have small chafing dishes, use them to keep the warm sauces up to temperature. This is a convivial feast, perfect for a special celebration with good friends. If you have a microwave, you may facilitate the preparation by steaming the vegetables in advance. Let them cool, and then arrange them beautifully on individual plates. Cover tightly with cling film. At serving time, microwave each plate to heat the vegetables through. Do not let them overcook, however.

LARDER LASAGNE

Serves 6
271 Calories per serving
7 g fat

This vegetarian dish is easily made from larder and freezer staples, yet the result is quite good. It can be made ahead and refrigerated for a day if desired – in fact the flavour improves under these circumstances.

---

1 bag (1 lb/450 g) frozen ratatouille vegetables (do not thaw)
Approx. 2 pts/1,200 ml stock
3 large Spanish onions, cut in half and sliced into thin half-moons
3 cloves garlic, crushed
4 tablespoons tomato paste
⅕ pt/120 ml chopped parsley
1 tablespoon fresh thyme (¼ teaspoon dried)
1 tablespoon chopped fresh basil (¼ teaspoon dried)
1 tablespoon fresh oregano (¼ teaspoon dried)

Salt, freshly ground pepper and cayenne pepper to taste
Approx. ¼ lb/112 g lasagne sheets (the kind that need no precooking)
¾ lb/338 g low-fat quark
5 tablespoons skimmed milk
Freshly grated nutmeg to taste
5 oz/140 g shredded low-fat Mozzarella cheese
7 tablespoons grated Parmesan cheese

---

1   Combine the *frozen* vegetables and 8 fl oz/240 ml stock in a deep heavy non-reactive frying pan. Bring to a boil, reduce heat and simmer, covered, for about 15 minutes.
2   Stir, and simmer, uncovered, for 15 minutes more.
3   Meanwhile, sauté the onions and garlic in ⅖ pt/120 ml stock according to the Slim Cuisine technique. When they are meltingly tender and amber brown, set aside.
4   Stir the sautéed onions, the tomato paste and the herbs and spices into the ratatouille mixture. Simmer, stirring occasionally for an additional 15 minutes until thick. If during this time it becomes too dry, and begins to stick, add a bit more stock.

5   Preheat the oven to 400° F (200° C/Gas Mark 6).

6   Pour 3–4 fl oz/120 ml of stock onto the surface of a non-reactive 9 × 13 in (23 × 33 cm) baking dish. Place a layer of lasagne sheets in the stock. Turn them to thoroughly wet them with stock.

7   Mix together the quark, milk, nutmeg, Mozzarella cheese and 4 tablespoons of Parmesan.

8   Spread half the ratatouille over the pasta. Spread half the cheese mixture over the ratatouille. Top with another layer of pasta.

9   Spread on an even layer of the remaining ratatouille. Spread the remaining cheese over this, mixing it in with the ratatouille as you spread. Sprinkle evenly with the last 2 tablespoons of Parmesan. Pour 4–5 fl oz/150 ml of stock over the top. (The baking dish can be refrigerated at this point for baking on the following day.) Bring to room temperature before baking.

10   Bake, uncovered, for 35 minutes.

FARMER'S OMELETTE

Serves 4
146 Calories per serving
7 g fat

Eggs are low in calories, full of high-quality protein and a fine collection of vitamins and minerals, but the yolks are, alas, high fat. One egg, once in a while, won't hurt, but don't make a habit of it. Save this for an occasional special weekend breakfast.

1 large baking potato, unpeeled, coarsely diced	1–2 fl oz/60 ml red wine (optional)
1 large onion, chopped	2–3 tablespoons parsley, chopped
3 cloves garlic, crushed	4 eggs
6–8 fl oz/240 ml stock	Freshly ground pepper
	2 tablespoons grated Parmesan cheese

1   Combine the potato, onion, garlic and stock in a frying pan. Bring to a boil, cover and boil for five minutes.

2   Uncover, reduce heat and simmer until the stock is almost gone and the vegetables are tender and beginning to brown. Pour in 1 oz/30 ml or so of wine or a splash of stock. Stir and scrape up browned bits. Transfer mixture to a large, non-stick omelette pan.

3   Preheat the grill. Beat the eggs with freshly ground pepper and Parmesan cheese. Pour over potato mixture. Let cook over medium heat without stirring for a few seconds until the eggs begin to set on the bottom.

4   With a flexible plastic spatula, lift the edges of the omelette away from the pan, and tilt the pan so that the uncooked egg flows beneath the cooked portion. Continue doing this all around the pan until the omelette is almost completely set, but soft and runny in the centre.

5   Place under the grill for 2–3 minutes to set and very lightly brown the top. Serve at once, in wedges, straight from the omelette pan.

RAJMAA – RED KIDNEY BEANS

Makes 2 pts/1,200 ml
Serves 8
111 Calories per serving
0.4 g fat

This dish is adapted from a family recipe of Shashi Rattan. I have substituted the Slim Cuisine Curry technique for her traditional ones.

---

2 large onions, coarsely chopped
1 pt/600 ml vegetable stock
2 teaspoons minced ginger
1 clove garlic, crushed
½ teaspoon ground cumin
½ teaspoon ground cinnamon
½ teaspoon ground coriander
Dash of ground cloves and cayenne
1 bay leaf
4 green cardamom pods, lightly crushed

1 large tin tomatoes (1 lb 12 oz/ 784 g)
2 tins (15 oz/420 g each) well rinsed and drained kidney beans
Salt to taste
½ pt/300 ml water or vegetable stock
Chopped fresh coriander (optional)

---

1   Separate the segments of the onion pieces and spread them in a heavy, non-stick, frying pan. Add *no* liquid or fat. Heat the frying pan gently. Cook at moderate heat, without stirring, for 7–10 minutes, until the onions are sizzling, speckled with dark amber, and beginning to stick to the pan.

2   Stir in 10 fl oz/300 ml of stock and let it bubble up, stirring up the browned deposits in the pan with a wooden spoon as it bubbles. Stir in the ginger, garlic and spices. Turn the heat

down a bit and simmer, stirring frequently, until the mixture is very thick (not at all soupy), and the onions and spices are 'frying' in their own juices. Don't rush this step, it is essential that the spices should not have a raw harsh taste. Taste. Cook very gently for a few more minutes if necessary.

3   Crush tomatoes with your hands and add them with their juices to the onions. Simmer for 3–4 minutes.

4   Add the beans, salt and remaining stock or water. Simmer briskly for 15–20 minutes until thick and savoury. Taste and adjust seasonings. Serve garnished with chopped coriander if desired.

Pasta and Sauces

'In the course of civilization's long and erratic march,
no other discovery has done more than or possibly
as much as pasta has to promote man's happiness.'

Marcella Hazan, *The Classic Italian Cook Book*, 1973

Slurping in the spaghetti (we never called it 'pasta' in those days) was one of the gastronomic glories of my American childhood. The long, luscious strands were inevitably buried under unsophisticated oceans of tomato sauce and there were always a few meatballs along to round things out nicely. Thinking of those comforting, sloppy meals of long ago makes me mistily nostalgic and ravenously hungry.

Here to assuage both physical and psychic hungers, are grown-up versions of those fondly remembered spaghetti feasts. Fat and Calories have been drastically cut, and ingredients and techniques have been upgraded to match the hard-won sophistication of adulthood, but these dishes still satisfy me (as they will you) in those cosy dim recesses of the soul that only *spaghetti* can reach.

Pasta Guidelines

For the sake of nutrient density, choose wholegrain pastas. In delicatessens and supermarkets, there is a gorgeous array of shapes and sizes from tiny wheels and shells to long, ribbon-like tagliatelli and flat, broad lasagne. If you grew up on white pasta and suspect that the wholewheat variety is pure stodge, you are in for a pleasant surprise. It is delicate in both taste and texture and its gentle brown colour is a lovely contrast to the brilliantly hued sauces into which it will be nestled. Cooking pasta perfectly is easy if you know the rules:

1   Bring plenty of lightly salted water to a rolling boil; at least 5 pts/3,000 ml of water per lb/450 g of pasta. If you are stingy with the water, the pasta will be gummy.
2   When the water is violently boiling, add the pasta, stirring with a wooden spoon as you do so. Long pasta such as spaghetti, linguine, etc. should be separated with the spoon as it begins to cook.
3   Stir frequently as it boils so that the pieces do not clump together. *Never* put the lid on the pot!
4   Do not overcook your pasta or you will end up with mush. Cook it until it is *al dente* (to the tooth). In other words, the pasta should be slightly resistant to the bite. Not at all raw, of course, but not at all mushy either. Begin fishing out pieces to taste – test early enough to avoid overcooking. (Use the timing suggested on the package as a guideline only.)
5   Have a large colander waiting in the sink. When the pasta is *just* done, don't dawdle. Use oven gloves and extreme care. Drain it quickly into the colander, combine it with its sauce, and serve *at once*.

PASTA SHELLS ALFREDO

Serves 5
284 Calories per serving
2.6 g fat
(traditional pasta Alfredo: 707 Calories per serving, 30 g fat)

Here is a dramatic example of the Calorie savings made possible by substituting dairy products. This supremely comforting dish is normally made with tons of butter and cream. Standard operating procedure for foodies in dire emotional straits (a recalcitrant lover, perhaps, or problems with the inland revenue) is to boil up some pasta shells, toss them hot and steaming into butter, double cream and grated Parmesan cheese, and to eat them blissfully with a large spoon. The consumption of this dish may cause your emotional troubles to fade temporarily into obscurity, but what does it do to your arteries and your avoirdupois? Nothing good! You will find the Slim Cuisine version of this comfort food just as delicious and even more comforting than the original. (You have the extra comfort of knowing that you are not harming your body.) This recipe may be multiplied or reduced as needed.

---

*10 oz/280 g pasta shells (or use
    tagliatelli or fettucini)*
*8 oz/224 g skimmed-milk quark, at
    room temperature*

*5 fl oz/150 ml skimmed milk, at
    room temperature*
*3 tablespoons freshly grated
    Parmesan cheese*
Freshly ground pepper to taste

---

1   Cook pasta to the *al dente* stage.
2   Meanwhile, scrape quark into a large, warm bowl. With a wooden spoon, beat in the skimmed milk and grated cheese.
3   Drain the pasta, and immediately toss it into the quark mixture. Grind in some pepper if desired, and serve at once.

Elegant Variation:

Toss some slivered smoked salmon into the pasta with the other ingredients, or add baked garlic purée (see page 30) and a handful of chopped fresh herbs (chives, parsley, basil).

LASAGNE

Serves 8
294 Calories per serving
6 g fat
(traditional lasagne: 2,136 Calories per serving)

The tastiest lasagne is made with a bolognese sauce that is based on crumbled Italian sausage meat. The sausage is a combination of pork shoulder, anise seed and crushed chillies. It's delicious but distressingly high in fat. Here I have eliminated the high fat level, but kept the unique Italian sausage taste.

---

1 recipe Bolognese Sauce (see page 102)
3 small baked aubergines, peeled, seeded (if the seeds are large) and chopped (see page 32)
½–1 tablespoon anise or fennel seeds
1–2 good pinches crushed dried chillies

1 lb/450 g low-fat quark
4 oz/112 g Mozzarella cheese, shredded
5 fl oz/150 ml skimmed milk
10 tablespoons Parmesan cheese
10 fl oz/300 ml stock
5 oz/140 g lasagne sheets, green or white (the kind that need no precooking)

---

1   Make the Bolognese sauce, adding the chopped flesh of the aubergine, the anise seeds and the crushed chillies before simmering the sauce. It should be well seasoned.
2   In a bowl, stir together the quark, Mozzarella cheese, milk and 7 tablespoons Parmesan cheese.
3   Preheat the oven to 400° F (200° C/Gas Mark 6).
4   Warm the stock. Pour 5 fl oz/150 ml of the stock in a 9 in/23 cm-square, 2½ in/6.4 cm-deep non-reactive baking dish. Pour the rest of the warm stock into a shallow dish.
5   Place a single layer of lasagne sheets in the stock in the baking dish. (Turn them to wet them thoroughly with the stock.)
6   Cover with ⅓ of the Bolognese sauce. Spread half the cheese mixture over the sauce. Dip some lasagne sheets into the warm stock in the shallow dish, turning them to wet them thoroughly. Spread in an even layer over the cheese.
7   Repeat, making another layer of sauce, cheese and lasagne sheets.
8   Top with the remaining sauce and an even sprinkling of the remaining Parmesan cheese.
9   Place a baking sheet on the oven floor to catch splatters and ease cleaning up. Bake the lasagne, uncovered, in the lower half of the oven for 1 hour. Let stand for 15 minutes before serving. This freezes well.

CHICKEN LASAGNE

Serves 8 generously
280 Calories per serving
4.46 g fat

I love the spice and herb combination in this dish: allspice, tarragon and a hint of soy sauce. Chicken Lasagne is delicious with a chicken that you poach yourself, a ready-cooked chicken from the super-market, or a smoked chicken.

---

5 peppers (mixed yellow and green) peeled and chopped (see page 162)
3 medium onions, finely chopped
2 cloves garlic, minced
1 lb/450 g mushrooms, quartered
1 pt/600 ml stock
4 fl oz/120 ml dry white wine
2 dashes soy sauce
½ teaspoon allspice
½ teaspoon dried tarragon
Freshly ground pepper to taste
2 tablespoons tomato paste

Shredded or diced meat from 1 small (2–2½ lb) poached or smoked chicken. (Make sure all fat, gristle and skin is discarded.)
1 lb/450 g skimmed-milk quark
3 oz/84 g part-skimmed Mozzarella cheese, shredded
5 tablespoons grated Parmesan cheese
4 fl oz/120 ml skimmed milk
7 oz lasagne sheets (the kind that need no pre-cooking)

---

1   Combine peppers, onions, garlic, mushrooms, 8 oz/300 ml stock, wine, soy sauce and seasonings in a large, non-stick frying pan. Stir to combine very well. Bring to a boil. Simmer briskly until the vegetables are tender and the liquid is greatly reduced and syrupy. Lower the heat a bit and cook gently, stirring occasionally, while the vegetables 'fry' in their own juices.
2   When the mixture is very thick and not at all soupy, stir in the tomato paste. Remove from the heat and stir in the chicken. Taste and adjust the seasonings. Set aside.
3   Stir together the quark, Mozzarella cheese, 3 tablespoons of Parmesan cheese and the milk. Set aside.
4   Choose a shallow, non-reactive 9 in/23 cm-square baking dish. Pour 4 fl oz/120 ml of warm stock into dish. Pour 3 oz/90 ml of warm stock into an extra shallow dish and keep it at hand.
5   Put an even layer of uncooked lasagne sheets in the shallow baking dish, turning them to wet them thoroughly. Cover with half the chicken mixture.
6   Dip more lasagne sheets in the stock in the extra dish, turning them to wet them. Put an even layer of the wet sheets over the chicken mixture. Cover with half the quark mixture.

7   Dip more lasagne sheets in the extra stock and put them in an even layer over the quark. Spread over the remaining chicken mixture. Spread the remaining quark mixture on top, mixing it in with the chicken mixture as you spread. Sprinkle 2 tablespoons of grated Parmesan evenly over the top. Pour 4 fl oz/ 120 ml of stock evenly over the baking dish, letting it flow down the sides.

8   Bake at 400° F (200° C/Gas Mark 6), for 45 minutes until browned and bubbly, and almost all the liquid is absorbed. Put the baking dish on a rack and let it sit for 15 minutes before cutting and serving. The rest of the liquid will be absorbed and the lasagne will cut nicely into neat squares.

The lasagne may be refrigerated for several days or frozen. If desired, cut into serving pieces and freeze in small microwave dishes, covered in cling film. At serving time, pierce the cling film in several places and microwave on full power for 4 minutes.

HUNGARIAN GREEN SAUCE

Makes 1 pt/600 ml of sauce
95 Calories per 5 fl oz/150 ml serving
0.7 g fat

The first time I made this delicate, pale green sauce, I was so pleased with myself that I walked around in a happy daze for the rest of the day. Serve the sauce with pasta, steamed fish, or Mushroom Ravioli (see page 53). Present it on a black, dark red, white or clear glass plate for maximum effect.

1½ lb/675 g green beans, trimmed	Pinch or two of cayenne pepper
5 shallots, halved and thinly sliced	2 fl oz/60 ml dry vermouth
1 large clove garlic, minced	6 fl oz/180 ml rich stock
1 teaspoon dried basil	Salt and freshly ground pepper to
1 teaspoon sweet Hungarian	taste
paprika	4 oz/112 g quark

1   Steam the green beans until very tender. Set aside.
2   Combine shallots, garlic, basil, paprika, cayenne pepper, vermouth and 2 fl oz/60 ml stock in a small frying pan. Boil, stirring occasionally, until the mixture is almost dry. Set aside.
3   Combine the beans, shallot infusion, remaining stock and quark in a liquidizer and purée.
4   Rub the purée through a sieve into a saucepan. Heat it gently. Taste and adjust seasonings.

PESTO

Makes 12 fl oz
9 Calories per teaspoon
0.4 g fat
(traditional pesto: 31 Calories per teaspoon, 3 g fat)

Pesto is a vividly coloured and flavoured thick Italian basil sauce, almost a paste. It is very good served tossed into hot pasta. Traditionally, pesto is made with plenty of olive oil. I have eliminated the oil altogether. I love this lower-fat version of the pungent Italian sauce even more than the classic one. To serve it as a very elegant starter, cook some small pasta shells *al dente*. Drain, rinse in cold water and drain very well. With a small spoon, stuff each shell with pesto (it sounds fussy, but it is really very easy and very fast). Arrange on a bed of radicchio leaves.

¾ pt/450 ml torn basil leaves	*½ lb/225 g quark or fromage blanc*
½ pt/300 ml roughly chopped	*cream cheese (see page 27)*
parsley	*Purée from 2 heads of baked garlic*
5 tablespoons freshly grated	*(or, for a stronger taste, several*
Parmesan cheese	*cloves of raw garlic)*
1 oz/28 g pine nuts	*Salt and freshly ground pepper to*
	taste

---

1   Combine all ingredients in the container of a food processor.
2   Process to a thick paste. Scrape into a bowl and refrigerate. If your quark is very fresh to begin with, the sauce will keep for a week.

Note: If fresh basil is unavailable, do not substitute dried. Make Parsley Pesto, Dill Pesto, or Spinach Pesto by substituting any of those greens for the elusive basil. If you use dill, omit the Parmesan. Dill Pesto is the perfect accompaniment to cold poached salmon.

More Suggestions for Serving Pesto:
1   Fill poached mushroom caps (see page 52) with Pesto. Arrange on juicy, ripe, sliced summer tomatoes. Garnish with whole basil leaves.
2   Toss the Pesto with linguine, fettucini or penne. Serve with Veal Meatballs (see page 90) or Italian Sausage Balls (see pages 94–5).
3   Toss fettucini or linguine with both Pesto and Tomato Sauce (see page 151). Add Sautéed Mushrooms (see page 26) if you wish.

4 Serve Pesto with slices of smoked salmon or spread on smoked salmon sandwiches.
5 Serve pasta with Bolognese Sauce (see page 102). Put a good dollop of Pesto on top of each serving.

RED PEPPER SAUCE

Makes 1½ pts/900 ml
50 Calories per 5 fl oz/140 ml serving
0.3 g fat

This is a rich, crimson, thick pasta sauce with a vivid and lively taste. It packs a large flavour wallop with only 5 Calories per tablespoon! In addition to pasta, the sauce is lovely with steamed vegetables. For each serving, spoon some of the hot sauce in the centre of a white or clear glass plate. Surround with a neat mound of vegetables that have been steamed until they are crisp-tender. Try peeled, trimmed asparagus, cauliflower florets, trimmed spring onions or green beans. To turn this combination into a hearty main dish, add grilled meatballs (see page 89). If you want a smoky taste, grill the peppers (see page 32) instead of simmering them in stock.

---

10 red bell peppers, coarsely
  chopped
12 fl oz/360 ml stock
Salt, freshly ground black pepper
  and cayenne pepper to taste

Onion-Herb Infusion, using
thyme, basil or tarragon (see
page 24)

---

1 Combine the peppers and stock in a deep, heavy frying pan. Bring to the boil. Cover, reduce heat and simmer for 20–30 minutes until tender.
2 Season with salt and peppers. Cool.
3 Purée the mixture in a liquidizer or food processor. Strain through a sieve or strainer, rubbing it through with a rubber spatula or wooden spoon. The skins, which are tough, will be left behind. Discard them.
4 Put the purée into a saucepan. Stir in the infusion. Simmer for 30 minutes. Taste and adjust seasoning. This sauce will keep in the refrigerator for a week. It also freezes well.

Variations:

CREAMY RED PEPPER SAUCE

58 Calories per 5 fl oz/140 ml serving
0.4 g fat

Prepare sauce as before. Just before serving, stir in 3–4 tablespoons skimmed-milk quark. Stir and cook over low heat until smooth, creamy and heated through. Serve at once. This is particularly good with pasta.

TOMATO-PEPPER SAUCE

37 Calories per 5 fl oz/140 g serving
0.2 g fat

Combine Red Pepper Sauce with Tomato Sauce (see page 151).

PASTA PRIMAVERA

300 Calories per serving
3.6 g fat

Toss *al dente* pasta with Red Pepper Sauce; a tablespoon of chopped sun-dried tomatoes rinsed in red wine and drained (optional, see page 45); Pesto (see page 145); Stir-'Fried' Courgettes in stock (see page 159); and Steamed Asparagus, cut into 1 in/2.5 cm pieces. Rush, steaming hot, to the table.

HELEN'S TERRACOTTA SAUCE

Makes 1 pt/600 ml
58 Calories per 4 fl oz serving
0.5 g fat

I developed this sauce while my 3-year-old godson, Natty Bumpo, was staying with us. He and Helen Bray, his beloved nanny, helped to taste-test it during his three-week visit. The colour is a warm terracotta, the texture rough and chunky and the taste rich. Serve with pasta, fish, pan-sautéed chicken or steamed cauliflower.

1 lb mushrooms, quartered
2 onions, chopped
2 large red peppers, chopped
2 cloves garlic, crushed
1 large carrot, peeled and coarsely
    grated
Approx. 2 pts vegetable stock

¼ pt dry white wine
2 dashes soy sauce
½ teaspoon dried tarragon
½ teaspoon allspice
2 tablespoons tomato paste
Salt and freshly ground pepper to
    taste

1   Combine mushrooms, onions, peppers, garlic, carrot, 8 fl
    oz/300 ml stock, wine, soy sauce, tarragon and allspice in a
    large, non-stick frying pan. Stir to combine very well. Bring to
    a boil, reduce heat somewhat, and simmer briskly until the
    vegetables are tender and the liquid is greatly reduced and
    syrupy. Lower the heat and let the vegetables 'fry' in their own
    juices, stirring occasionally.
2   Stir in the tomato paste. Season with salt and pepper. Cool
    slightly.
3   Purée the mixture in a liquidizer or food processor. Push half
    of the purée through a non-reactive sieve. Combine the sieved
    and unsieved mixtures. Refrigerate until needed.
4   To reheat, pour into a saucepan and thin with 2–3 tablespoons
    stock or water. Simmer gently, stirring occasionally. Be *very*
    careful because the sauce is thick and is prone to violent,
    volcanic bubbling.

Pasta Pronto

Pasta suppers are fun. They provide plenty of scope for exuberant
improvisation and they can often be prepared in less than half an
hour. When you have worked late and are ready for a sumptuous
and comforting meal, although you haven't had the time to plan for
it, think of pasta. Put the water on to boil and choose your pasta
type from the selection you are sure to have in the larder. Then
open the fridge and explore. Some of the most fascinating pasta
sauces are born of a good leftover rummage. My favourite? Leftover Chilli Con Carne (see page 101), Tomato Sauce (see page 151)
and Sautéed Mushrooms (see page 26) combined in a saucepan
with a handful of raisins and a few pine nuts. Let it simmer gently
while the pasta (penne works well) cooks. When the penne is
done, toss with the improvised sauce and hey presto! Pasta ala
Picadillo.

PENNY'S PENNE

Serves 8
299 Calories per serving
3.2 g fat

I invented this pasta dish for my mother-in-law when she came to visit. It was such a success that I made it again for my assistant's, Penny Roseveare's, birthday lunch. Save this for very special occasions – it's glorious.

½ lb/225 g large mushrooms, cut
  into chunks
1 large red or yellow pepper, peeled
  and cut into pieces (see page 162)
1 onion, chopped
3 cloves garlic, chopped
6 fl oz/180 ml dry red wine
6 fl oz/180 ml stock
Dash or 2 soy sauce
1 tin (14 oz) chopped tomatoes
Piece Parmesan cheese rind
¼ teaspoon each: dried thyme,
  oregano, basil

1 tablespoon sun-dried tomato paste
  (see page 45) or 1 tablespoon
  tomato paste
Salt and freshly ground pepper to taste
1 lb/450 g penne or pennoni
  (tubular, quill-shaped pasta)
8 oz/224 g mangetout, fresh, or
  frozen and thawed, destrung
4 fl oz/120 ml Slim Cuisine Pesto
  (see page 145)
4–6 oz/150 g smoked chicken,
  sliced thin and cut into ½ in/1.3
  cm pieces

---

1   Preheat the oven to its lowest points. Put a large serving bowl in the oven to keep warm.

2   Combine the mushrooms, pepper, onion, garlic, wine, stock and soy sauce in a heavy, non-reactive frying pan. Simmer briskly, stirring occasionally, until the vegetables are tender and the liquid is thick and syrupy.

3   Stir in the tomatoes, Parmesan rind, herbs, tomato paste, salt and pepper. Simmer gently, uncovered, for 15 minutes. Stir occasionally.

4   Meanwhile, cook the penne or pennoni in plenty of boiling, salted water until *al dente*.

5   While the penne is cooking, put the mangetout into a sieve or strainer. Just before the penne is done, dip the sieve with the mangetout into the boiling pasta water. If the mangetout are frozen and thawed, leave in the boiling water for 2 seconds, if fresh for 10 seconds.

6   Drain the pasta in a colander. Pour it into the warm bowl. Immediately toss in the mangetout and the chicken. Toss with 2 spoons so that everything is well mixed. Stir in the tomato – mushroom sauce. Toss well to distribute it. Toss in the pesto. Everything must be very well combined. Rush to the table and serve at once.

LEMONY PASTA SHELLS

Serves 1
295 Calories per serving
1 g fat

When you want to whip up something in a hurry that is comforting yet low-Calorie, try this soothing pasta pilaff. (Broken-up angel hair pasta can be substituted for the shells, for an occasional change.) This amount makes a happy culinary indulgence for one, but you may comfort a companion or two, as well, by doubling or tripling the recipe. As a variation, try adding garlic purée from roasted garlic to the infusion. For a more substantial dish, add veal meatballs before the final simmering. (The meatball version is a great family pleaser.)

1 recipe Onion-Herb Infusion (see page 24)
2 oz/56 g tiny wholewheat pasta shells

8 fl oz/240 ml boiling stock
Freshly ground pepper to taste
Fresh lemon juice to taste

1   Heat the infusion in a pot. Toss the pasta with the infusion until it is well combined.
2   Stir in the hot stock and grind in some pepper. Cover and simmer over very low heat for 10–12 minutes or until the liquid is almost absorbed. (It will be just a bit soupy.)
3   Squeeze in the lemon juice (I like to use the juice of 1 small lemon), stir and serve at once.

'So what happens when we eat food? Well, the answer is that after the food is eaten, if it is rich in Calories and cream sauces and so on, we argue about the bill. Then after that we get fat. Then the fat gets deposited on women's hips, which causes more arguments, and in men's coronary arteries which ends arguments. There now, that wasn't very complex, was it?'

Robert Buckman, *Punch*, April 1987

LEMON CREAM SAUCE

Makes 16 fl oz/480 ml
51 Calories per 4 fl oz/120 ml serving
0.1 g fat

A delicate pasta sauce with a fresh, lemony taste. Drain the fromage frais in a cheesecloth-lined sieve for a few hours before using it in this recipe. To elevate this to ambrosia, toss in some slivered smoked salmon.

⅕ pt/120 ml water
Grated rind of ½ lemon
4 tablespoons fresh lemon juice
Salt and freshly ground pepper to
    taste

2 tablespoons buttermilk, at room
    temperature
⅖ pt/240 ml drained low-fat
    fromage frais, at room
    temperature

---

1   Combine water, lemon rind, lemon juice, salt and pepper in a small frying pan or saucepan. Boil, uncovered, until reduced to about 4 tablespoons. Cool.
2   Beat the lemon infusion and the buttermilk into the fromage blanc. (This may be made a few days in advance and stored in the refrigerator. The flavour will intensify.) Bring to room temperature before using. Toss into hot, freshly cooked spaghetti, tagliatelli or shells.

TOMATO SAUCE

Makes 1½ pts/900 ml
19 Calories per 4 fl oz/120 ml serving
0.0 g fat
(traditional tomato sauce: 156 Calories per serving, 7.7 g fat)

If you think it is impossible to make a good tomato sauce without olive oil or butter, think again! This is fast, easy to make and lovely on pasta, or pizza. Sautéed chopped red and yellow peppers and sautéed mushrooms (see page 26) may be added. It freezes very well.

---

3 shallots, finely chopped
2 cloves garlic, peeled and crushed
Pinch cayenne pepper
6 fl oz/180 ml stock
6 fl oz/180 ml dry red wine, white
    wine or vermouth
1 tablespoon chopped fresh parsley

1 tablespoon each chopped fresh
    basil, thyme and oregano or ¼
    teaspoon each dried basil, thyme
    and oregano
3 tins (14 oz/392 g each) chopped
    tomatoes
Parmesan cheese rind
Salt and freshly ground pepper to
    taste
2 tablespoons tomato paste

---

1   Combine shallots, garlic, cayenne, stock, wine and herbs in a heavy frying pan. Bring to the boil. Reduce heat and simmer briskly until almost all the liquid has been evaporated. Season to taste.

2   Stir in the drained tomatoes (you may crush them with your hands), Parmesan rind, salt and pepper. Simmer, partially covered, for 15 minutes. Stir in the tomato paste and simmer for 5 minutes more. Taste and adjust seasonings. Discard the Parmesan rind. Serve with pasta or on pizza, or try it spooned into jacket potatoes.

Variation:

SHAWM'S SMOOTH TOMATO SAUCE

My son loves homemade tomato sauce, but hates lumps in his food. Should you have such a family member or friend, let this sauce cool somewhat, and then purée it in the liquidizer. Rub it through a non-reactive sieve. It's convenient to make this sauce in bulk, and then store it in small tubs in the freezer.

HERBED AUBERGINE SAUCE

Makes 1 pt/600 ml
93 Calories per 5 fl oz/150 ml serving
0.5 g fat

A hearty, spicy sauce that is particularly good tossed with penne, ziti or rotelli.

2 aubergines, approx. ½ lb/225 g each, baked (see page 32)	4 peppers, 2 yellow and 2 red, peeled and cut into thin strips (see page 162)
5 shallots, peeled, halved and thinly sliced	1 tin (14 oz/397 g) chopped Italian tomatoes
½–1 tablespoon fennel seeds	
1 tablespoon rosemary leaves, crumbled	1–2 tablespoons roasted garlic purée (see page 00)
1 teaspoon crushed chillies (or to taste)	1 tablespoon tomato paste
4 fl oz/120 ml dry red wine	Salt and freshly ground pepper to taste
10 fl oz/300 ml chicken or vegetable stock	1 piece Parmesan rind

1   Peel the aubergines and cut them in half. Discard any seeds that seem large and tough. Chop the flesh coarsely. Put into a large, heavy, non-reactive frying pan. Set aside.

2   In another frying pan, combine the shallots, fennel seeds and rosemary, chillies, wine and 4 fl oz/120 ml of stock. Boil briskly, stirring frequently, until almost dry. Add this mixture to the aubergine.
3   Heat 2 fl oz/60 ml of stock in the frying pan in which you cooked the shallot mixture. When very hot, dump in the peppers. Stir-'fry' until the liquid is almost gone. Scrape the peppers into the pan with the aubergine.
4   Stir in the remaining ingredients, including the remaining stock. Simmer for 10–15 minutes until thick and savoury. Taste and adjust seasonings. Serve with pasta or as a filling for jacket potatoes or potato cases (see page 172) or use as a filling in a vegetarian lasagne.

Variation:

CREAMY AUBERGINE SAUCE

104 Calories per serving
0.6 g fat

Stir in some skimmed-milk quark and heat gently.

More Pasta Ideas

For a quick and delicious meal try any of the following tossed with the pasta of your choice.

Any vegetable (or combination of several vegetables) trimmed, cut up and stir-'fried' in a combination of stock and wine. Add chopped herbs and some Slim Cuisine Sautéed Onions if you wish.

Sautéed Mushrooms, alone or sautéed with peeled chopped yellow and red peppers and onions (see page 26).

Tzatziki (see page 57).

Room-temperature yoghurt mixed with salt and pepper and chopped fresh herbs. Add a clove or two of crushed garlic marinated in a bit of white wine vinegar if desired.

Room-temperature low-fat cottage cheese or quark thinned a bit with skimmed milk, seasoned with ground cinnamon, caraway seeds or poppy seeds. If desired, add some thinly sliced cabbage stir-'fried' in stock until just barely tender.

Hummus (see page 59).

Salsa (see page 170).

Tomato Sauce (see page 151) to which you have added drained, flaked tuna in brine, crushed raw garlic or baked garlic purée, a few capers and a handful of chopped parsley. Add a dash or two of tabasco sauce.

Tomato Sauce in which you have simmered stock-sautéed slivered carrots, cooked kidney beans, chick peas and chopped parsley.

Browned Onions (see page 23) and Stir-'Fried' Peppers (see page 162).

Mustard Cream (see page 170).

Pesto, Tomato Sauce, Italian Sweet and Sour Courgettes (see page 160) and Sautéed Mushrooms.

Vegetable Side Dishes

'Even today, well-brought up English girls are
taught by their mothers to boil all veggies for at least
a month and a half, just in case one of the dinner
guests turns up without his teeth.'

Calvin Trillin, *Third Helpings*, 1983

Steam your vegetables, sauté them, stir-'fry', bake or braise them, but *please* don't boil them to death. Boiling robs them of many nutrients, and causes small children to utter loud retching noises when presented with a plate of the miserably flabby things. What a glorious profusion of vegetables can be found in British markets as the seasons change. From the humble roots to slim, elegant asparagus, from familiar sprouts to exotic fennel, from celery to celery root – experiment, taste, revel in the variety.

VEGETABLE BHAJI

Serves 6
117 Calories per serving
0.6 g fat

This Bhaji packs lots of nutrition into a very low-calorie, low-fat dish. The sauce is a thick and rich purée of onions, peppers, mushrooms and carrots. Serve the Bhaji with Raita (see page 183) and Basmati Rice for a wonderfully satisfying main dish, or serve it as part of an array of curries. I have also served it tossed into pasta.

2 large onions, cut into eighths
Approx. 1 pt/600 ml stock
2 cloves garlic, crushed
1½ teaspoons ground cumin
1½ teaspoons ground coriander
½ teaspoon allspice
½ teaspoon ground turmeric
½ teaspoon ground ginger
¼ teaspoon cayenne pepper (or to taste)
1 small red and one small yellow pepper, chopped
3 carrots, peeled and coarsely chopped
¾ lb/338 g mushrooms, quartered
1 tablespoon tomato paste
2 medium boiling potatoes, peeled and cut into 1½ in/3.75 cm pieces
1 large cauliflower, trimmed and broken into large florets
½ large lemon
Salt to taste
½ lb/225 g French beans, trimmed and cut into 1½ in/3.75 cm lengths

1   Separate the segments of the onion pieces and spread them in a heavy, non-stick frying pan. Add *no* liquid or fat. Heat the frying pan gently. Cook at moderate heat, without stirring, for 7–10 minutes, until the onions are sizzling, speckled with dark amber, and beginning to stick to the pan.
2   Stir in 10 fl oz/300 ml of stock and let it bubble up, stirring up the browned deposits in the pan with a wooden spoon as it bubbles. Stir in the garlic, spices, peppers, mushrooms and

carrots. Turn the heat down a bit and simmer, stirring frequently, until the mixture is very thick (not at all soupy), and the vegetables and spices are 'frying' in their own juices. Don't rush this step – it is essential that the spices should not have a raw harsh taste. Cook very gently for a few more minutes. Stir in the tomato paste.

3   Purée half the mixture in a liquidizer and push it through a sieve. Combine the puréed and unpuréed mixture in the pan.

4   Add the potatoes and cauliflower to the pan. Toss everything together very well. Pour in stock to reach about ⅓ of the way up the sides of the pan. Squeeze the juice of ½ lemon over the contents of the pan. Season with salt. Bring to a boil.

5   Reduce heat, cover the pan and simmer for 15 minutes. Stir in beans and continue simmering for 5 minutes more or until all the vegetables are tender.

Note: This reheats very well. If you plan to cook ahead, undercook the Bhaji slightly so that the vegetables do not turn to mush when they are reheated.

BRAISED CAULIFLOWER WITH FENNEL SEEDS

Serves 6
40 Calories per serving
0.2 g fat

This is a sensational vegetable dish with enough interesting play of flavours to make it the star of a meal. It can be served hot or cold, but I like it best at room temperature, when all the splendid flavour seems to explode in the mouth. It is not a visually beautiful dish, so line a bowl with curly lettuce leaves, and spoon in the cauliflower, then garnish with parsley.

1 large clove garlic, peeled	*1 large or 2 small cauliflowers,*
¼ pt/150 ml fresh parsley	*broken into florets*
1 tablespoon rosemary leaves	*6 fl oz/180 ml stock*
½–1 tablespoon fennel seeds	*1 heaped tablespoon tomato paste*
½ pt/300 ml browned onions or	*Salt and freshly ground pepper to*
sautéed onions (see page 23)	*taste*
2 tablespoons red wine vinegar	*Chopped parsley*

1   Chop together the garlic, parsley, rosemary and fennel. Set aside.

2 Place the browned onions in a deep, heavy frying pan. Heat until the onions begin to sizzle and stick to the frying pan. Pour in the wine vinegar and boil, stirring and scraping up the browned bits with a wooden spoon.

3 When the liquid is almost gone, stir in the garlic mixture. Add the cauliflower. Toss everything together until it is well combined.

4 Whisk together the stock and the tomato paste. Season with salt and pepper. Pour over the cauliflower and stir again. Bring to the boil, cover, reduce heat and simmer until the cauliflower is very tender but not disintegrating (about ½ hour in all). Cool to room temperature and serve. Garnish liberally with chopped parsley. This may be prepared 1–2 days ahead, in fact the flavour will improve. Store in the refrigerator. Bring to room temperature before serving. Add the parsley garnish just before serving.

GRATIN OF BAKED VEGETABLES

Serves 6
80 Calories per serving
1.5 g fat

Warming, comforting and an attractive, glowing orange. The gratin freezes very well, and, when frozen, reheats beautifully in the microwave.

---

5 white turnips, peeled	*Salt and freshly ground pepper to*
6 medium carrots, peeled	*taste*
Purée from one head baked garlic	*4 tablespoons freshly grated*
(see page 29)	*Parmesan cheese*
2–3 tablespoons buttermilk	

---

1 Preheat the oven to 425° F (220° C/Gas Mark 7).

2 Loosely wrap the whole turnips in foil, shiny side in, crimping the package well so that no steam escapes. Wrap the carrots in similar fashion. Bake for 1 hour in the preheated oven, until the vegetables are very tender.

3 Unwrap. Trip stem and root ends. Place the turnips in a bowl and mash them with a potato masher. Scrape into the bowl of a food processor. Cut the trimmed carrots into chunks. Add to the turnips. Add the garlic purée.

4 Process the vegetables until they are smooth. Add buttermilk and process until blended. Season to taste.

5   Scrape the mixture into a small non-reactive gratin dish or shallow baking dish. Smooth the top and sprinkle with Parmesan. (The dish may be prepared ahead of time to this point. Refrigerate, well covered, until needed. It will keep for up to two days. Bring to room temperature before proceeding.)
6   Reduce oven temperature to 350° F (175° C/Gas Mark 4). Bake uncovered for 30–45 minutes until browned on top and thoroughly hot.

Variations:

Parsnips or swedes may be substituted for the carrots or turnips. Potatoes may be added, although with potatoes, do not use a food processor. Purée by pushing through a sieve or a food mill. Seasonings may be varied as well. Try ground allspice, cinnamon, cumin or mace.

STIR-'FRIED' COURGETTES WITH LIME AND CUMIN

Serves 6
14 Calories per serving
0.1 g fat

This recipe is a prime example of how to stir-'fry', without oil. Try leftovers served cold with a sprinkling of interesting wine vinegar.

6–8 small courgettes	Salt and freshly ground pepper to
4 fl oz/120 ml stock	taste
Generous pinch of ground cumin	Juice of 1 lime

1   Wash and trim the courgettes but do not peel them. Cut them in half and then into strips about 2 in/5 cm long and ½ in/1.3 cm wide.
2   Pour the stock into a heavy, non-reactive frying pan. Bring to a boil.
3   Dump in the courgettes. Grind in a generous amount of pepper, and sprinkle in the cumin. With two wooden spoons, constantly toss and turn the vegetables over high heat until they are crisp-tender, and the stock has cooked down to almost nothing. Squeeze in the lime juice, season lightly with salt to taste and let the courgettes stir-'fry' for a minute or so in their own juices. Serve at once.

159

STIR-'FRIED' COURGETTES WITH GARLIC AND GINGER

13 Calories per serving
1 g fat

Mince a clove of garlic and a thin slice of peeled ginger root. Put them in the frying pan with the stock and 1 fl oz/30 ml dry sherry and let boil for a few seconds before dumping in the courgettes. Omit the pepper and the lime juice. If desired, sprinkle with some chopped fresh coriander before serving.

ITALIAN SWEET AND SOUR COURGETTES

40 Calories per serving
1.6 g fat

Add 3 cloves of minced garlic to the stock and let boil for a few seconds. Dump in the courgettes, freshly ground pepper, 2 tablespoons each of raisins, drained, rinsed capers, and pine kernels, and the juice of 1 lime. Just before serving, stir in some finely chopped parsley. Serve hot or cold.

STIR-'FRIED' CAULIFLOWER

Serves 6
25 Calories per serving
0.1 g fat

Cauliflower is very good steamed until crisp-tender. It is even better stir-'fried' in stock.

---

1 large head cauliflower	*1 clove garlic, minced (optional)*
6 fl oz/180 ml stock	*Salt and freshly ground pepper to*
Dash of fresh lemon juice	*taste*

---

1   Cut off and discard the tough end of the cauliflower stalk. Discard the leaves. Separate the cauliflower in florets.

Mexican baked beans with tiny Mexican meatballs (page 91) and chilaquiles (tortilla pieces and chicken in a piquant sauce) (page 129).

2   Pour the stock and lemon juice into a wide, heavy, non-reactive frying pan or wok. Heat to simmering. Toss in the cauliflower, optional garlic, and salt and pepper, cover and simmer for 3 minutes.

3   Uncover. Turn the heat to high. Stir and toss the florets in the boiling stock until the stock is almost gone and the cauliflower is crisp-tender. Serve at once.

STEAMED ASPARAGUS

52 Calories per 10 spears of asparagus
0.4 g fat

Please take the time to peel your asparagus before cooking it – what a difference it makes! This asparagus is so good that in season I often eat a large platter for dinner all by itself. Believe me, it is worth the peeling. If you want to get fancy, serve this asparagus as a first course with Red or Yellow Pepper Sauce (see page 146). Put a puddle of the sauce on a pretty plate, and surround the puddle with the beautiful green stalks. For a main course, add Veal Meatballs.

Fresh asparagus stalks, washed

---

1   Cut off the tough woody bottom portion of each stalk. With a swivel-bladed vegetable peeler, peel each stalk from the bottom up to the buds. If you are not going to cook them at once, stand them in a glass of water as if they were a bunch of flowers.

2   Place the stalks in a steamer basket. Steam over boiling water for 3–7 minutes (depending on size) until crisp-tender. To test, pull out one stalk with tongs. Hold it up. It should just bend a *little* bit.

Clockwise from lower right: spinach-stuffed goose skirt steak with wine sauce (page 109) and stock-sautéed root vegetables (page 112); chick-pea-potato salad (page 187); pasta with terracotta sauce (page 147); fresh mango sorbet with berries (page 205).

STIR-'FRIED' ASPARAGUS

56 Calories per 10 spears asparagus
0.4 g fat

Fresh asparagus stalks, washed	*Pinch thyme and tarragon*
3–4 fl oz/120 ml stock	*Salt and freshly ground pepper to*
½ lime	*taste*

---

1   Trim and peel the asparagus (see previous recipe) and cut into
    1 in/2.5 cm lengths. Heat 3–4 fl oz/120 ml of stock in a
    non-reactive wok or frying pan. Throw in the asparagus and
    toss and turn in the hot stock for about 2 minutes (use two
    wooden spoons or spatulas).
2   Squeeze in the juice of ½ a lime, add a pinch each of thyme and
    tarragon and salt and freshly ground pepper to taste. Keep
    stir-frying for a few more moments, until crisp-tender (more
    crisp than tender). Serve at once.

STIR-'FRIED' PEPPERS

17 Calories per serving
0.1 g fat

Peeling the peppers sounds tedious, but it is not much more
difficult than peeling a carrot, and the textural difference between a
peeled and unpeeled pepper is a big one. And without the skin, the
peppers, when cooked in stock, produce a thick and delicious
sauce. They are much more digestible when peeled, too. This is a
very rich-tasting, colourful and soul-satisfying vegetable dish, well
worth the peeling time. Eat it as a vegetable accompaniment, try it
tossed into pasta, or serve it as a sauce with Goose Skirt Steak (see
page 106) or Pan-Sautéed Chicken Breasts (see page 114).

---

3 red peppers	*6 fl oz/180 ml stock*
3 yellow peppers	*Freshly ground pepper to taste*

---

1   Cut the peppers in half, lengthwise. Remove the stem, the
    seeds and the ribs. Cut the halves into their natural sections.
2   Peel each pepper piece with a swivel-bladed vegetable peeler.
    Cut each piece into strips about ½ in/1.3 cm wide.
3   Heat the stock in a heavy frying pan. When very hot, toss in
    the peppers and grind in some black pepper. With two
    wooden spoons, toss and turn the peppers in the hot stock
    until the liquid has cooked down considerably. Turn down the

heat a bit and 'fry' them for a few minutes in their own juices, until they are very tender, and the pepper juices have formed a thick sauce. Serve at once with their delicious juices, or serve at room temperature. This dish may be made in advance and rewarmed later or the next day.

CREAMED SPINACH

Serves 4
61 Calories per serving
0.6 g fat

---

4 oz/112 g low-fat quark at room temperature

2–3 tablespoons skimmed milk, at room temperature
Purée from 1 head roasted garlic
Salt and pepper to taste
Pinch nutmeg
1 lb/450 g spinach, very well washed, stemmed and cut into strips

---

1 Stir together the quark and milk. Stir in the garlic, salt, pepper and nutmeg.
2 Put the spinach into a large, non-reactive pot. Cook, stirring, in the water that clings to its leaves, until limp and greatly reduced in volume but still bright green. Drain in a colander.
3 Fold the spinach and the quark mixture together. Serve at once.

Baked Beetroot

Make the most of beetroots by baking them. No other cooking method brings out their sweetness and flavour as well, and the texture will be very good indeed. Trim the greens away, and wrap the whole, unpeeled beetroots in heavy-duty foil, shiny side in. (3–4 beetroots may go in one package). Bake at 400° F (200° C/Gas Mark 6) for 1–2 hours, until tender. (Timing depends on age and size.) Use a skewer for testing doneness. The skewer should go in easily but the beetroots should not be mushy. Cool, then trim and slip off the skins. Serve sliced with a sauce of 2–3 parts yoghurt to one part Dijon mustard (less mustard if you don't like spicy food) mixed with a clove of crushed garlic, that has marinated for a few minutes in a little bit of wine vinegar. Season with salt, freshly ground pepper and a pinch or two of sugar.

'As for beetroots, their excuse for being is the fine colour they add to pale dishes.'

Alice B. Toklas, *The Alice B. Toklas Cookbook*, 1954

BEETROOT PURÉE

Makes 1 pt/600 ml sauce
12 Calories per tablespoon
0 g fat

Ruby red and textural, this is an unusual and interesting purée. Serve it mounded in poached button mushrooms (see page 52) or spoon dollops onto the wide ends of chicory leaves. Or serve it as a spread on black bread, with smoked salmon if you're feeling luxurious. The mushroom and chicory versions make a visually stunning party dish, especially if they are arranged on a black plate. I like to keep this purée for snacking. It makes a dandy between-meal nibble.

---

2 lb/900 g baked beetroots (see page 163), or use ready-cooked beetroots from the supermarket (if they are very vinegary, reduce the amount of vinegar in the recipe)

8 tablespoons fromage blanc
1–2 cloves garlic
Salt and freshly ground pepper
1½–2 tablespoons wine vinegar

---

1 Slip the skins off the beetroots and allow them to cool. Cut into chunks.
2 Combine the cooled beetroots and all remaining ingredients in the food processor. Process until puréed (the texture will remain somewhat rough). Taste and adjust seasonings – it should be quite peppery with a nice balance of sweet and sour. Chill.

Variation:
Stir in grated, squeezed dry, horseradish instead of garlic.

Seasoning Vegetables

Melted butter or margarine are the classic toppings for steamed vegetables. I lived for many years in the American South where vegetables are seasoned with bacon or fatback. In the Mediterranean countries the vegetables glisten with a coating of olive oil. None of these are appropriate to the Slim Cuisine regime. What to do?

Try this. Boil good-quality vegetable or chicken stock until greatly reduced and syrupy. Toss with the vegetables. Even better, mix the stock with dry red or white wine, dry vermouth, or dry sherry, interesting wine vinegar, or lemon or lime juice, and then boil down until syrupy. Add herbs or spices before you boil, but season with salt, to taste, *after* the boiling, or it will be much too salty.

STEAMED BROCCOLI

41 Calories per stalk of broccoli
0.3 g fat

Broccoli is so awful when boiled until flabby. Try it steamed briefly and rejoice in its special taste and texture.

1   Wash the head of broccoli very well. Split it into single stalks. Cut off and discard the tough ends. Peel the stalks up to the flowers with a paring knife.
2   Spread the broccoli evenly in a steamer. If you love garlic, sprinkle some chopped cloves of this over the broccoli. Cover and steam over boiling water for 5–7 minutes until crisp-tender (test with a cake tester or a tooth pick). Serve at once with wedges of lemon or lime.
3   If the broccoli is to be served cold, refresh under running cold water to stop the cooking and set the vivid green colour.

Variation:
Cut the florets off the stalks. Save the stalks to serve on the next day. Steam the florets for 3–4 minutes over boiling water. Serve hot or cold, with lemon juice or reduced stock (see above).

To serve the stalks, peel them and slice ¼ inch thick and steam until tender or stir-'fry' in a small amount of stock and lemon juice until crisp-tender (see page 159 for stir-'fry' procedures).

BRAISED FENNEL

Serves 4
52 Calories per serving
1.8 g fat

Fennel looks a lot like celery and tastes like mild liquorice. Braised fennel is very good as a companion to meats, or as part of a vegetable dinner.

2 bulbs fennel, trimmed and cut in
  half lengthwise, then each half
  cut into wedges approx. ½ in/
  1.3 cm wide
Freshly ground pepper

4 fl oz/120 ml stock
3 tablespoons Parmesan cheese

1   Preheat oven to 350° F (180° C/Gas Mark 4).
2   Arrange fennel in one layer (cut side down) in a baking dish.
     Pour over 4 fl oz/120 ml stock. Season with pepper. Sprinkle
     evenly with 3 tablespoons Parmesan cheese.
3   Bake uncovered for 45 minutes. The fennel will become mel-
     tingly tender and the stock will have cooked almost com-
     pletely away, leaving a rich glaze. Serve at once.

BRAISED MUSHROOMS

71 Calories per ½ lb/224 g mushrooms
0.43 g fat

Serve as a vegetable accompaniment or a starter. It works well on a
buffet at a drinks party. Because the soy sauce is salty, you won't
want to add any salt as you cook the mushrooms.

3 lb/1,350 g button mushrooms,
  cleaned
16 fl oz/480 ml salt-free vegetable
  or chicken stock
4 fl oz/120 ml dry sherry
4 tablespoons soy sauce

1 tablespoon sugar
2 large cloves garlic, peeled and
  crushed
2 thin slices ginger root, peeled and
  chopped

1   Place the mushrooms in a deep, heavy non-reactive pot. Add
     all remaining ingredients.
2   Bring to a boil. Reduce heat to a brisk simmer and cook,
     uncovered, stirring occasionally, until the mushrooms are
     deep mahogany brown and the liquid is greatly reduced.
3   With a slotted spoon, remove the mushrooms to a bowl. Boil
     the remaining liquid until reduced by half. Pour over the
     mushrooms. Serve hot or at room temperature. If they are to
     be part of a buffet, have cocktail picks nearby for spearing.

MUSHROOM RAGOUT

60 Calories per ½ lb/224 g mushrooms
1 g fat

Serve this mushroom-lover's special as a vegetable side dish or as a starter. The more kinds of mushrooms you can find, the nicer this will be.

A variety of fresh mushrooms (look for fresh shiitake, chestnut and oyster mushrooms in addition to the ordinary cultivated ones; trim the tough stems from shiitakes before using them)
Freshly ground pepper to taste

Dash of soy sauce
Dry sherry or dry vermouth
Stock
Purée from roasted garlic (optional)
Toast Cups (recipe follows)
  (optional)

1   Clean mushrooms well, cut into quarters or eighths (depending on size) and combine with seasonings and liquids in a large non-stick frying pan.
2   Cook briskly until the liquid in the pan is greatly reduced.
3   Stir in the garlic purée. Cook, stirring, for a minute or so more, until the mushrooms are tender, and in a syrupy sauce. Taste and correct seasonings.
4   Spoon individual servings of the ragout into toast cups and serve at once.

TOAST CUPS

31 Calories per toast cup
0.3 g fat

Use a non-stick patty tin (or muffin tin) and a thin-sliced loaf of bread. Trim the crusts from each slice of bread. Roll over each slice with a rolling pin. Gently fit each slice into one of the cups of the tin. Bake at 400°F (200°C/Gas Mark 6) for 10–15 minutes until lightly browned.

Variation:

MUSHROOM SALAD

As a lower-calorie alternative, add some good wine vinegar (optional) to the finished ragout and serve in lettuce cups or chicory leaves (approx. 2 calories per lettuce leaf, 0 g fat).

DUXELLES

Makes 1 pt/600 ml
172 Calories per pt/600 ml
3 g fat
(4.3 Calories per tablespoon, 0.2 g fat)

Duxelles is a kind of mushroom hash, with a very intense mushroom taste. It is useful in all sorts of preparations, so it pays to make it in quantity and store it in the refrigerator or freezer. At its most basic, try it spread thickly on bread, or stirred into sauces or soups. Better still, try it in Baked Potatoes (see page 170) or in Ravioli (see page 53). For the most intense mushroom flavour use a combination of types of fresh mushrooms. I use shiitakes, trimmed of their tough stems, chestnut mushrooms, oyster mushrooms and the usual cultivated ones.

1½ lb/675 g mixed mushrooms,
  cleaned well
8 fl oz/240 ml vegetable stock
4 fl oz/120 ml sherry
Several dashes soy sauce

1 teaspoon dried tarragon,
  crumbled
Salt and freshly ground pepper to
  taste

---

1   Chop the mushrooms very, very finely. This is best done in a food processor if you have one. Quarter the mushrooms and put them into the food processor bowl. Pulse on and off until very finely chopped. You will need to do this in 2 or more batches.
2   Empty all the chopped mushrooms into a deep, non-reactive frying pan. Add the stock, sherry, soy sauce and tarragon. Stir it all up. The mushrooms will be barely moistened but it doesn't matter.
3   Cook over moderate heat, stirring occasionally until the mushrooms have rendered quite a bit of liquid. Turn the heat up a bit and simmer briskly, stirring occasionally until the mushrooms are very dark, very thick and quite dry. Season to taste. Store in the refrigerator until needed.

'Free! Free at last! His mouth watered at the thought of the meals he was going to have in the next few days. Potatoes and Martinis and warm buttered rolls and all the other forbidden foods.'

Robert Silverberg, *The Iron Chancellor*, 1958

BAKED POTATOES

173 Calories per large (8-oz) potato
0.2 g fat

Jacket potatoes are comforting, sustaining and deeply satisfying. I've always thought that they were much too good to be relegated to the status of a mere accompaniment. For a fun, informal and easy dinner, try serving a big napkin-lined basket of jacket potatoes, surrounded by an array of bowls containing all those things that go so delectably well in the potatoes. Remember, the potatoes themselves are low-fat, low-Calorie and high-nutrition. When stuffing the potatoes, beware of wicked things like butter, soured cream and high-fat cheeses. Instead try a dollop of yoghurt or fromage blanc, a splash of buttermilk, a modest shower of freshly grated Parmesan cheese, a squeeze of lemon juice, a scattering of herbs, a mound of Duxelles (see page 168), a deluge of homemade Salsa (see page 170) or a dab or so of Dijon mustard. Whatever you do, don't neglect to eat the skin. It is chock-full of nutrients, and the contrast of crunchy skin against tender flesh is part of what makes a jacket potato so special.

Large, unblemished baking potatoes (try Wiljas or King Edwards if you can find them. Wiljas bake to a very creamy texture and *King Edwards to a very floury texture. Both are very good for the soul)*

---

1   Preheat the oven to 425° F (220° C/Gas Mark 7).
2   Scrub the potatoes and pierce them in several places with a thin skewer or the prongs of a fork. Never wrap the potatoes in foil, or they will steam rather than bake.
3   Bake directly on the oven shelf for about 1¼ hours or until the potatoes yield softly to a gentle squeeze. (Arm yourself with an ovenglove before you squeeze!)
4   Split the potatoes by perforating them lengthwise and breadthwise with the prongs of a fork and squeezing, so that the tender potato flesh comes surging up. Sprinkle on a tiny bit of salt and a generous grinding of fresh black pepper and you have one of the earth's great foods at its simplest. Or serve with the accompaniments suggested above.

Note: Baked potatoes make the most wonderful mashed potatoes. Scoop out the potato flesh (and save the skins for a private nibble). Put the potatoes through a ricer or, for a homelier (and much easier) effect, mash with a potato masher. With a wooden spoon, beat some buttermilk into the hot potatoes. Season with a touch of salt and plenty of freshly ground pepper.

169

SALSA FOR BAKED POTATOES

Makes ⅘ pt/480 ml
261 Calories entire recipe
0.1 g fat
8.1 Calories per tablespoon

This cold Mexican sauce spooned into steaming hot jacket potatoes is very good indeed. I also like to toss the cold Salsa with hot pasta. It makes a ravishing 'hot as summer, cold as winter' effect.

2 large tins (1 lb 12 oz/784 g each) Italian tomatoes (or use peeled and seeded fresh tomatoes in the summer when 'real' tomatoes are available) Finely chopped fresh chilli peppers, to taste, or chopped tinned chillies or a mixture	2 fl oz/60 ml red wine vinegar 2 cloves garlic, minced 2 tablespoons chopped fresh parsley 1 tablespoon chopped fresh coriander

1   Drain the tomatoes and chop them (save the juice for soups).
2   Combine all ingredients in a non-reactive bowl. Chill.

Note: To turn this into a cold soup, use the tomato liquid as well. If you wish, add chopped baked peppers (see page 31).

DUXELLES CREAM FOR BAKED POTATOES

7 Calories per tablespoon
0.1 g fat

1 recipe Duxelles (mushroom 'hash', see page 168)	½ lb/225 g quark 2–3 tablespoons buttermilk

Stir the Duxelles into the quark. Beat in the buttermilk.

MUSTARD CREAM FOR BAKED POTATOES

13 Calories per tablespoon
0.3 g fat

2 tablespoons buttermilk ¼ lb/113 g yoghurt cheese (see page 27)	2 tablespoons Dijon mustard 1 tablespoon chopped fresh parsley 1 tablespoon chopped fresh chives

Combine all ingredients in a processor and process until perfectly smooth. Failing a processor, beat with a wooden spoon.

BORSCHT POTATOES

222 Calories per potato
0.3 g fat

One of the classic ways to serve Borscht (Russian beetroot soup) is cold, with a steaming-hot, floury potato in it. The hot/cold contrast is marvellous. I have reversed the classic. It is still quite marvellous.

Large baked potatoes   *Dill fronds (optional)*
Beetroot Purée (see page 164)

1   With a fork, perforate the hot potatoes lengthwise and breadthwise and squeeze open.
2   Pile a generous dollop of cold Beetroot Purée on each potato. Top each with a dill frond. Serve at once.

STUFFED POTATOES

Serves 2–4
170 Calories per half-potato
2.3 g fat

Serve these as a main course with Braised Mushrooms (page 166) and Chinese-Style Cabbage Salad (page 189) or Tomato-Basil Salad (page 185) or serve as an accompaniment to Peppered Steak (page 107). Serve 2–3 halves per person as a main course, 1–2 as an accompaniment. This recipe works beautifully with King Edward potatoes.

1 large head garlic   *4 tablespoons grated Parmesan*
2 large baking potatoes   *cheese*
4 oz/112 g quark   *Salt and freshly ground pepper to*
Approx. 6 fl oz/180 ml buttermilk   *taste*
                                       Cayenne pepper to taste

1   Preheat the oven to 400° F (200° C/Gas Mark 6).
2   Prepare the garlic heads for baking (page 29). Place the foil-wrapped garlic in the oven. Bake for ¾–1 hour.
3   Pierce the potatoes in several places with a skewer or fork. Let

them bake directly on the oven shelf for 1–1¼ hours, while the garlic bakes.

4   Meanwhile, beat together the remaining ingredients. When the garlic is done squeeze the softened garlic pulp into the cheese mixture.

5   When the potatoes are done, cut them in half lengthwise. Scoop the potato flesh into a bowl. Be very careful to leave the potato shells intact. Mash the potatoes with a masher. With a wooden spoon, beat in the cheese-garlic mixture. Beat in more buttermilk, if necessary, to make a very creamy mixture. Adjust seasonings.

6   Pile the potato mixture into the potato shells. Place them in a baking dish. (The recipe may be prepared up to this point and refrigerated. Bring back to room temperature before continuing.)

7   Place the baking dish in the hot oven. Bake for 10–15 minutes. If they have not browned lightly on the top at this point, put briefly under the grill. Serve at once.

'No-one has feared developing leprosy from eating French Fries . . . but we all know that Fries make us fat (or fatter), cause blemishes, induce indigestion, nourish ulcers, and make havoc of cholesterol counts. Yet everybody keeps stuffing them down . . . the greasier and more awful the better.'

James Villas, *Esquire Magazine*, 1974

POTATO CASES

30 Calories per potato case
0 g fat

Potato Cases are perfect if you are craving crisps or chips. They are crunchy and just right for potato-snack needs. If you wish, cut them in quarters instead of halves. They will bake faster, and be more like finger food.

Large Baking Potatoes

---

1   Preheat the oven to 400° F (220° C/Gas Mark 7).
2   Scrub the potatoes and halve them lengthwise.
3   With a teaspoon or a melon-baller, scoop out the insides, leaving a shell about ¼ in/0.6 cm thick. Save the scraps for another use (see note).

4   Bake directly on the oven rack for 25–35 minutes, until golden brown and very crisp. Serve at once – as they are; with dips; or filled with a savoury mixture.

Note: Don't you dare throw the potato scraps away. Use them to make a wonderful gratin. It may be made at once, refrigerated, and reheated at a later date.

Potato Scrap Gratin

1   Scoop the potatoes right into a saucepan and add enough stock to barely cover. Season with a bit of salt and plenty of pepper. If you wish you may add a bit of grated nutmeg or a pinch of ground cumin and cayenne pepper. Simmer covered until tender. Do not drain.
2   Mash roughly (just to chop up the pieces, not to purée them) right in the pot, with a potato masher. Spread into a gratin dish. Dribble on a bit of skimmed milk, and sprinkle with some Parmesan. Bake, in a hot oven, uncovered, for 50–60 minutes, until bubbly and well browned on top. Serve at once, or refrigerate for reheating in a day or two.

POTATO GRATIN

Serves 8
100 Calories per serving
1 g fat

This gratin is a symphony of texture and taste. The starch in the potatoes, the flavourful stock and the grated cheese form a thick, creamy sauce that binds the tender potato slices under a crusty top – sheer heaven!

---

1 large clove garlic	*Salt and freshly ground pepper*
4 large unpeeled baking potatoes	*³⁄₅ pt/360 ml of vegetable or chicken*
4 tablespoons freshly grated	*stock*
Parmesan cheese	

---

1   Preheat the oven to 400° F (200° C/Gas Mark 6).
2   Peel the garlic clove and split it. Rub a 9 × 13 in/23 × 33 cm oval gratin dish with the split sides of the garlic.
3   Slice the potatoes paper-thin. Do not soak them in water at any time. Slice just before using.
4   Layer ⅓ of the potato slices in the gratin dish and sprinkle evenly with Parmesan cheese, salt and pepper. Pour ⅓ of the stock over the potatoes.

173

5   Repeat twice more. With a broad spatula, press the top layer down into the liquid.
6   Bake in the preheated oven for approximately 1½ hours until the potatoes are tender, the liquid has cooked down to a thick sauce and the top is brown and crusty.

Note: The gratin can be made the morning or the day before and reheated in a microwave or a 375° F (190° C/Gas Mark 5) oven.

Variations:
1   Layer Browned Onions (see page 23) with the potatoes, cheese and stock. Cook as directed.
2   Mix 1 tablespoon Dijon mustard with 4 oz/120 ml whisky. Stir in the stock. Proceed and bake as directed.
3   Layer Sautéed Mushrooms (see page 26) with the potatoes. For pure luxury, add soaked, drained, dried mushrooms and use some of the strained mushroom liquor for part of the stock.

GRATIN OF BAKED POTATOES, ONIONS AND GARLIC

Serves 8
130 Calories per serving
1 g fat

I invented this dish for a book I wrote a few years ago, *Comfort Food*. I have cut out the high-fat ingredients of the original recipe, but it is still one of the most comforting recipes I know.

---

4 large baking potatoes, baked and mashed (save skins for another use)
Purée from 2 large heads of baked garlic (see page 29)
2 large Spanish onions, baked and puréed (see page 31)
Salt and freshly ground pepper to taste
2–3 tablespoons buttermilk

4–5 tablespoons freshly grated Parmesan cheese
1 tablespoon instant dried skimmed-milk powder
3 tablespoons stock

---

1   Preheat oven to 325° F (165° C/Gas Mark 3).
2   Combine the potato, garlic, onions, salt and pepper. Beat with a wooden spoon. Beat in the buttermilk.
3   Scrape the mixture into a gratin dish. Smooth the top and sprinkle with the cheese. (The recipe may be prepared in

advance to this stage and refrigerated, covered, for a few days. Bring to room temperature before proceeding.) Whisk together the milk powder and the stock. Dribble the mixture evenly over the top of the potatoes. Bake uncovered for 35–45 minutes, until brown, bubbly and thoroughly hot. Serve at once. (This is very exciting when it is cold, too.)

'If you have formed the habit of checking on every new diet that comes along, you will find that mercifully, they all blur together, leaving you with only one definite piece of information: french-fried potatoes are out.'

Jean Kerr, *Please Don't Eat the Daisies*, 1958

CHIPS

173 Calories for chips from 1 large (8-oz) potato
0.2 g fat
(Traditional chips: 270 Calories per 8-oz potato, 13 g fat)

Why deprive yourself of crisps or chips? You can feast on these compelling munchies to your heart's content, if you use no fat. They are actually superior to the usual fat-laden kind, because as you munch, you taste *potato*, not a mouthful of grease and salt. The potatoes may be sliced thick (½ in/2.5 cm) or thin (¼ in/1.3 cm). The thin ones will be crisp and crunchy like crisps, the thicker ones will be brown and crunchy on the outside, and floury-tender within, like chips. This recipe works very well with large Maris Pipers.

Baking potatoes	Warm stock

1   Preheat the oven to 425° F (220° C/Gas Mark 7).
2   Don't bother to peel the potatoes. Cut them crosswise into ¼–½ in (1.3–2.5 cm) slices. Cut each slice in half.
3   Put a little bit of warm stock in a large bowl along with the potatoes and stir them around well with your hands so that they are coated with the warm stock.
4   You will need one or two flat baking sheets with non-stick coating. Spread the potatoes on the sheet(s) in one layer. Put them in the oven and leave them for ½ an hour.
5   Pull the potatoes out and with a spatula gently turn them. Bake in the oven for approximately another 5–15 minutes. (The timing depends on the thickness of the slices.) By this

time they should be browned, crunchy and puffed. Serve at once. (These may be sprinkled with a bit of salt if desired, but I find they don't really need it.)

ROAST POTATOES

Serves 4
138 Calories per serving

Melting tenderness and superb flavour with no fat at all. As they bake, the kitchen is filled with the most tantalizing aroma.

1 head fresh, firm garlic	Approx. 6 fl oz/180 ml stock
3 medium onions, halved and sliced into thin half-moons	Salt and freshly ground pepper to taste
8 medium new potatoes, unpeeled and cut in half	

1   Preheat oven to 400° F (200° C/Gas Mark 6).
2   Separate the head of garlic into cloves. Hit each clove smartly with a kitchen mallet. Remove and discard the skin. Scatter the crushed cloves and the onion slices on the bottom of a baking dish that will hold the halved potatoes in one layer.
3   Place the halved potatoes, cut sides down, on the bed of garlic and onions. Pour in stock to come about ¼ up the sides of the dish. Sprinkle salt and pepper evenly over all.
4   Bake uncovered for 1 hour, until the potatoes are tender, the onions beginning to brown and the liquid about gone. Serve piping hot. Encourage diners to mash the garlic, onion and potatoes together if they wish.

CURRIED ROAST POTATOES

Serves 4 as an accompaniment (100 Calories, 0.2 g fat), 2 as a main dish (200 Calories, 0.4 g fat)

With plenty of Raita (see page 183) these would make a good meal. No meat is needed.

1 large onion, cut in half and each half cut into eighths	½ teaspoon ground cayenne pepper
Approx. 15 fl oz/450 ml stock	1 clove garlic, crushed
1 thin slice ginger, minced	Salt and pepper to taste
1 teaspoon ground coriander	4 medium potatoes, unpeeled and quartered
1 teaspoon ground cumin	Wedges of fresh lime

1 Separate the segments of the onion pieces and spread them in a heavy, non-stick frying pan. Add *no* liquid or fat. Heat the frying pan gently. Cook at moderate heat, without stirring, for 7–10 minutes, until the onions are sizzling, speckled with dark amber, and beginning to stick to the pan.

2 Stir in 10 fl oz/300 ml of stock and let it bubble up, stirring up the browned deposits in the pan with a wooden spoon as it bubbles. Stir in the ginger, garlic and spices. Turn the heat down a bit and simmer, stirring frequently, until the mixture is very thick (not at all soupy), and the onions and spices are 'frying' in their own juices. Don't rush this step – it is essential that the spices should not have a raw, harsh taste. Taste. Cook very gently for a few more minutes if necessary.

3 Toss the potatoes into the mixture. Stir to combine everything very well. Scrape the potatoes and spices into a shallow baking dish that can hold them in one layer. Add the remaining stock.

4 Bake for 1 hour, stirring occasionally and adding a bit more stock as needed, until the potatoes are tender. The finished dish should be dry. Serve hot with wedges of lime.

MASHED POTATOES

85 Calories per 3½ oz/100 g
1 g fat

Nothing helps you drift into serene calm faster than a steaming bowlful of this magical food. Conventionally prepared, the mashed spuds are usually loaded with cream and butter, producing sensual pleasure as you eat, followed by guilt and fat the next day. Let's keep the sensual pleasure and eliminate the guilt and fat.

To make perfect mashed potatoes, choose large baking potatoes. They have a floury texture when cooked, and mash up into a fluffy, ethereal cloud. Avoid waxy boiling potatoes; they become a sticky mass when mashed. Boil the baking potatoes, in a covered pot of salted water to generously cover, until very tender but *not* falling apart. You will obtain the best results as far as taste and nutrition are concerned if the potatoes are boiled whole and unpeeled; but, if you are in a hurry, they may be peeled and quartered before boiling.

When the potatoes are tender, drain them in a colander. (If you love to bake bread, save the potato liquid. It is excellent for bread dough.) If the potatoes are whole and unpeeled, grasp with an oven glove and scrape off the skins with a table knife. Quarter them and return to the pot. If they were already peeled and quartered, simply return them to the pot directly after draining.

Cover the pot and shake it over low heat to toss the potatoes as they dry. For exceptionally fluffy, airy mashed potatoes, force them through a ricer into a warm bowl. For homelier, denser potatoes, use a potato masher, and mash them right in the pan over very low heat. Work the potatoes well with the masher. It is alright to leave in a lump or two, to prove that these are *real* mashed potatoes, but watch out for rampant lumpiness or they will be awful. Don't be tempted to use your food processor; you'll end up with a gluey mess.

When the potatoes are mashed or riced, season to taste with salt and pepper. (For a really interesting if unconventional taste, add a bit of ground cumin and cayenne pepper too.) With a wooden spoon, beat in a liberal amount of room-temperature buttermilk. A bit of freshly grated Parmesan cheese can be beaten in too if you wish. When the potatoes look creamy and luxurious, scrape them into a warm bowl, grab a *large* spoon, seat yourself in your favourite easy chair, and eat blissfully.

Variations:

1   Add one of the following vegetables to mashed potatoes (steam or bake the vegetables and use an equal weight of the vegetable and of potatoes):
      Mashed swedes
      Mashed parsnips
      Mashed turnips
      Mashed carrots
      Mashed celeriac
2   Or stir in:
      Browned onions (see page 23)
      Puréed, baked onion (see page 31)
      Baked garlic purée (see page 29)
      Medium-fat creamy goat cheese
      Chopped chives
3   Or, for a delectable potato experience, fill a bowl with mashed potatoes. Make a well in the potatoes with the back of a dessert spoon. Fill the well with Sautéed Mushrooms, or Mushroom Ragout (see page 167).
4   Or make a Mashed Potato Gratin: Mash the potatoes, beat in plenty of buttermilk and a bit of Parmesan, season with salt, freshly ground black pepper, a sprinkle of cayenne pepper and a couple of pinches of ground cumin. Spread in a gratin dish. Dribble a bit of skimmed milk evenly over the surface and sprinkle with some Parmesan. (It may be made in advance to this point and refrigerated. Bring to room temperature before proceeding.) Bake at 400°F (200°C/Gas Mark 6) for ¾–1 hour until puffed with a golden crust.

SPICY LENTILS

Makes 3.5 pts/2,100 ml
120 Calories per ¼ pt serving
0.4 g fat per ¼ pt serving

This makes *a lot* of lentils, but it freezes or refrigerates well and tastes so good upon reheating. If you wish, dilute the leftovers with plenty of stock to make a delicious soup.

---

2 large onions, cut into eighths
3 pts/1,800 ml stock
1 tablespoon minced fresh ginger
1 clove garlic, minced
1 teaspoon ground cinnamon
1 teaspoon ground coriander
Cayenne pepper to taste

1 lb/450 g brown lentils, washed
*   and picked over*
Salt
2 large limes
Chopped fresh coriander (optional)

---

1   Separate the segments of the onion pieces and spread them in a heavy, non-stick frying pan. Add *no* liquid or fat. Heat the frying pan gently. Cook at moderate heat, without stirring, for 7–10 minutes, until the onions are sizzling, speckled with dark amber, and beginning to stick to the pan.

2   Stir in 10 fl oz/300 ml of stock and let it bubble up, stirring up the browned deposits in the pan with a wooden spoon as it bubbles. Stir in the ginger, garlic and spices. Turn the heat down a bit and simmer, stirring frequently, until the mixture is very thick (not at all soupy), and the onions and spices are 'frying' in their own juices. Don't rush this step, as it is essential that the spices should not have a raw, harsh taste. Taste. Cook very gently for a few more minutes if necessary.

3   Add in the lentils. Stir so that they are coated with the onions and spices. Add some salt. Cut the limes in half. Squeeze the juice into the lentils. Add the squeezed halves to the pan. Pour in 2 pts/1,200 ml of stock.

4   Simmer, uncovered, for 10 minutes. Skim off foam as it comes to the surface.

5   Cover and simmer gently, stirring occasionally, for 45–50 minutes. Add more stock during this time as needed.

6   Taste the lentils. If they are not quite tender, add more stock and simmer for 15–20 minutes, until completely tender and the mixture is hot. Taste and add more salt and lime juice if necessary. Serve hot, garnished with coriander if desired.

179

Salads and Dressings

'Following her is Leonid, a young student who is
too shy to speak to Natasha but places a mixed
green salad on her doorstep every night.'

Woody Allen, *Without Feathers*, 1976

S alads often seduce dieters into outrageous over-indulgence. Although everyone knows that salads are perfect for chronic Calorie counters, it is easy to forget that lashings of thick, oily dressings, fried croutons and the like are the antithesis of diet food. Leave off the densely calorific components, and salads can be a dieter's salvation. And by replacing the sludgy, oil-laden dressings with delicate, low-fat ones, the salads will be aesthetically much more pleasing.

General Guidelines for Salad Dressings

Use the Slim Cuisine 'mayonnaise' dressings (see page 27) or drain low-fat fromage blanc or yoghurt for an hour in a cheese-cloth-lined sieve. Mix it with a splash of freshly squeezed lemon or orange juice or wine vinegar.

To this basic mixture may be added minced raw garlic or roasted garlic purée, chopped fresh herbs, ground spices, grated citrus zest, grated fresh ginger, minced shallots or spring onion, a dash of soy sauce or Worcestershire (look for reduced-salt Worcestershire in wholefood shops), Dijon mustard, a few dashes of tabasco sauce, minced capers, a dab of tomato paste (for a 'Russian' dressing) or grated horseradish. Choose the flavouring to complement the salad.

For a creamy, zesty dressing, try mixing 2–3 parts of drained low-fat yoghurt to one part Dijon mustard with a splash or two of interesting vinegar (balsamic, raspberry, sherry, herb, etc.). In fact, the more interesting vinegars, particularly sherry and balsamic, make good dressings all by themselves.

If you love to eat salad in restaurants, order them without dressings. Carry a small jar of your own dressing and apply it discreetly.

CREAMY SALAD DRESSING

6 Calories per tablespoon
0.1 g fat

Salads are full of fibre, low-fat, low-Calorie, vitamin- and mineral-packed veggies, and, alas, usually drenched in horrifically high-fat dressings. How nice to know that you can have your salad cream minus the fat by using Slim Cuisine 'mayonnaise' as a base.

Wine vinegar (use as interesting a vinegar as you can find and afford. Sherry, balsamic or raspberry vinegars are excellent. White wine tarragon vinegar works nicely too)	Buttermilk 'Mayonnaise' (see page 27)

Whisk the vinegar and a bit of buttermilk into the 'mayonnaise' in a thin stream until the consistency of single cream.

Vary this dressing to your taste with garlic, herbs, spices, etc. A specific example follows.

CREAMY HERB SALAD DRESSING

Makes 8 fl oz/240 ml dressing
10 Calories per tablespoon
0.2 g fat

Try this variation of the previous recipe on a special tossed salad – for instance, green and red lettuces tossed with chicory leaves, strips of red and yellow pepper, watercress and orange segments.

1/5 pt/120 ml yoghurt cream cheese 4 tablespoons buttermilk 1–2 tablespoons Dijon mustard 1½ tablespoons sherry vinegar	2 cloves crushed garlic (optional) 1/8 pt/75 ml fresh basil leaves Salt and freshly ground pepper to taste

1 Combine all the ingredients in the container of a food processor.
2 Process until smooth. Scrape into a jar, cover tightly and refrigerate until needed.

CUCUMBER RAITA

Makes approximately 1 pt/600 ml
34 Calories per 2 fl oz/60 ml serving
0.6 g fat

Always serve a cooling Raita (yoghurt salad) with your curries. Here are my favourites.

1 pt/600 ml low-fat yoghurt	Chopped fresh parsley
1 large cucumber, peeled, halved and seeded	Chopped fresh coriander
	Thinly sliced spring onions (green and white portions)
Salt and freshly ground pepper to taste	Chilli powder (optional)

1 Dump yoghurt into a bowl.
2 Grate the cucumber into the yoghurt.
3 Stir to combine. Season to taste with salt and pepper. Garnish generously with parsley, coriander and spring onions. Sprinkle on chilli powder if desired. Serve at once as an accompaniment to curries.

Variation:

Mix plenty of chopped fresh mint with yoghurt. Omit the cucumbers and the coriander.

ORANGE WATERCRESS SALAD

39 Calories per serving
0.3 g fat

This is a beautiful and refreshing salad, perfect for warm weather. Reckon on ½ an orange per person, a few sprigs of watercress and a teaspoon of dressing. For a stunning presentation, arrange the salad on clear glass plates.

Juicy, seedless oranges	Freshly ground pepper
Watercress (wash and shake dry)	½ teaspoon grated orange rind
Low-fat yoghurt, drained for about 1 hour	Pinch ground cumin

1 On a cutting board, slice the oranges thinly. With a paring knife, neatly remove the rind and white pith from each slice. Do not wipe away the orange juice that collects on the board.
2 Overlap the orange slices on half of a clear glass plate. Fan out the watercress on the lower half. Stir the orange juice that has collected on the cutting board into the drained yoghurt along with the pepper, orange rind and cumin. Either serve the dressing in a clear glass jug along with the salad, or pour a thin stripe of dressing down the centre of each row of orange slices, and serve the rest separately.

TOMATO-BASIL SALAD

33 Calories per serving
0.3 g fat

Tomato and basil form a heavenly culinary alliance. Make the most of this duo during the summer, when both are in glorious profusion. For a more substantial salad, alternate slices of tomato with slices of Italian part-skim Mozzarella cheese.

Ripe tomatoes	*Sherry vinegar or other good, mild*
Basil leaves, torn into shreds	*wine vinegar*
Salt and freshly ground pepper	

1   Neatly cut the stem out of the tomato. Slice them from stem to stern. Arrange the slices on a plate. Sprinkle lightly with salt and pepper.
2   Scatter the shredded basil over the tomatoes. Sprinkle on a modest amount of vinegar. Let stand for 10 minutes before serving.

MARINADED CUCUMBER SALAD

Serves 6
6 Calories per serving
0.1 g fat

A low-fat version of a classic Hungarian salad. The creamy variation on these cucumbers is especially good with grilled skirt steak or roasted chicken. Serve it on the same plate as the meat, so that the meat juices mingle with the salad.

2 large cucumbers, peeled	*½ teaspoon Hungarian paprika*
Salt	*Freshly ground pepper*
3 tablespoons white wine vinegar	*1 small clove garlic, crushed*
3 tablespoons cold water	*(optional)*
½ teaspoon caster sugar	

1   Slice the cucumber thinly into a colander. Toss lightly with salt. Let drain for ½ hour. Rinse and blot dry on paper towels.
2   Meanwhile, whisk together the vinegar, water, sugar, ¼ teaspoon of paprika, pepper and garlic. Mix this into the rinsed drained cucumbers. Chill for an hour or so before serving. Just before serving, sprinkle the remaining paprika over the top of the salad.

Creamy Variation
35 Calories per serving
0. g fat

After mixing the cucumbers with the dressing, blend in 8 fl oz/240 ml of low-fat fromage blanc. Chill, sprinkle with paprika and serve.

NEW YORK POTATO SALAD

Serves 10
123 Calories per serving
0.3 g fat
(traditonal potato salad:
273 Calories per serving, 18 g fat)

One of my favourite potato salads is New York Jewish delicatessen style. It is made with baking potatoes that mash up a bit when chopped. When mixed with the dressing they mash even more, so that the final texture is compellingly smooth and creamy. In fact, it is almost a mashed potato salad. Make it for a crowd, or store it in the refrigerator to nibble at through the week. It gets better each day.

---

3 lb/1,350 g baking potatoes
2 small carrots, peeled
1 small celery stalk
1 red pepper, peeled
1 yellow pepper, peeled

1 teaspoon sugar
Salt to taste
6 fl oz/180 ml Slim Cuisine
  'mayonnaise' (see note)

---

1   Put potatoes in enough lightly salted water to cover gener-ously and boil until tender. Drain and cool for a few minutes (they should still be warm when the dressing is added to them).
2   Grate 1 carrot, the celery and half of each pepper.
3   With a table knife, scrape the skins off the still-warm potatoes. Place the potatoes on a chopping board. With a hand chopper or a chef's knife, chop them. As you chop, they will mash slightly. Put them in a bowl.
4   Squeeze any accumulated liquid out of the grated vegetables. Add the vegetables to the potatoes. Sprinkle with sugar and salt. Mix lightly.
5   With a wooden spoon, fold in the mayonnaise. As you do so, the potatoes will mash even more. When well combined, refrigerate until serving time.

6   To serve, mound the salad on a platter. Chop the remaining pepper and grate the carrot. Garnish the salad all around its perimeter with the vegetables.

Note: Follow directions for Slim Cuisine 'mayonnaise' with this difference: use half low-fat yoghurt and half low-fat fromage frais.

CHICK PEA-POTATO SALAD

Serves 8
71 Calories per serving
0.4 g fat

This is a lively potato salad. The chick peas and potatoes complement each other so the quality of protein is high and, of course, the yogurt adds still more good protein. As a result the salad would be excellent as part of a vegetarian meal.

---

1 lb/450 g boiling potatoes
1 tin chick peas
2 tablespoons fresh lime juice
1 teaspoon soy sauce
½ teaspoon ground cumin
¼ teaspoon cayenne pepper (much less if you don't like things spicy)

3 spring onions, trimmed and sliced thinly
2 tablespoons chopped fresh parsley
3 tablespoons drained yoghurt
1 tablespoon buttermilk

---

1   Steam the potatoes until tender but not mushy. Cut into ½ in/1.3-cm cubes while still warm.
2   Drain and rinse the chick peas. Combine them in a bowl with the potatoes. Stir together the lime juice, soy sauce and spices. Add to the potatoes. Toss gently with 2 spoons so that they absorb the liquid. Stir in the spring onions and parsley.
3   Stir together the yoghurt and buttermilk. Gently fold the mixture into the potatoes.

FENNEL-PEPPER SALAD

Serves 4
42 Calories per serving
0.4 g fat

The liquorice crunchiness of fennel makes this salad exceptionally pleasing. Serve it as a separate course, either before or after the main dish.

1 medium head fennel, trimmed of tough outer layer and core, and sliced thin (save feathery leaves)	1 tablespoon capers, drained and rinsed
1 small red pepper, sliced thin	2 large cloves garlic
1 small yellow pepper, sliced thin	1 small bunch fresh parsley
¼ lb/113 g button mushrooms, cleaned well and sliced thin	2 fl oz/60 ml Slim Cuisine mayonnaise
	1–2 tablespoons buttermilk
	1 tablespoon wine vinegar

1   Combine the fennel, peppers, mushrooms and capers in a bowl.
2   Finely chop together the garlic and parsley. Toss it, along with the feathery fennel leaves, into the vegetables.
3   Whisk together the mayonnaise, buttermilk and vinegar. Toss the dressing with the salad, or pass it in a clear glass jug. Serve at once.

COLE SLAW

Serves 8
55 Calories per serving
0.5 g fat

There are infinite versions of cole slaw. Mine is extremely colourful and full of texture and contrasting flavour. If you own a food processor, the grating and slicing is child's play. This is particularly good for a buffet, a barbecue or a picnic.

½ small head red cabbage	2 tablespoons drained yoghurt (see page 27)
½ small head white cabbage	
3 small carrots, grated	3–4 tablespoons buttermilk
1 medium red pepper, cut into very thin strips	1 tablespoon German mustard
1 medium yellow pepper, cut into very thin strips	1 tablespoon white wine vinegar
	2 small cloves garlic
2 stalks celery, sliced thin	1 tablespoon chopped parsley
½ head fennel, trimmed and sliced thin	Salt and freshly ground pepper to taste
⅕ pt/120 ml grated white radish	

1   Cut the core out of the cabbage halves and trim away the tough outer leaves. With a chef's knife or with the slicing disk (not the grating disk) of a food processor, slice it into thin slices. Combine the cabbage with the rest of the vegetables.

2   Combine the remaining ingredients in the liquidizer. Blend until smooth. Toss this dressing with the vegetables. Let marinate for at least an hour before serving.

CHINESE-STYLE CABBAGE SALAD

Serves 4
58 Calories per serving
0.3 g fat

This is an approximation of the cabbage salad my friend Frank Ma used to serve me at his Chinese restaurant in Atlanta, Georgia. I have adapted it somewhat but the salad still has the authentic Chinese taste.

¾ lb/338 g green cabbage, shredded
2 large carrots, shredded
4 tablespoons fresh lime or lemon
*   juice*

1 teaspoon sugar
1 small clove garlic, crushed
Cayenne pepper to taste
1 tablespoon soy sauce

1   Combine cabbage and carrots in a large bowl.
2   Whisk together the remaining ingredients. Toss into the vegetables. Toss the salad with 2 spoons so that the cabbage is well coated with the dressing. Let stand for at least 15 minutes, stirring occasionally.

TABOULI

Serves 8
129 Calories per serving
0.6 g fat

Tabouli is a salad of herbs, tomatoes and grain. The colourful mixture is extraordinarily refreshing. The success of the dish depends on the tomatoes; they must be ripe and bursting with flavour. Tabouli goes very well with grilled fish, chicken or meat, or with lamb meatballs. And it makes a pretty addition to a salad buffet. Bulghur is available in most wholefood stores.

8 oz/224 g cracked wheat (bulghur)
4 fl oz/120 ml fresh lemon juice
2 bunches parsley, stemmed and
*   finely chopped*
1 bunch spring onions, trimmed
*   and finely chopped*

1 bunch fresh mint, finely chopped
2 lb/900 g skinned (see page 44)
*   ripe tomatoes (squeeze out seeds*
*   and juice) chopped*
Salt and freshly ground pepper to
*   taste*

1 Soak the wheat in cold water to cover. Use a large bowl as it will expand a great deal. After 30 minutes, squeeze the grains with your hands to drain them and place in a clean bowl.

2 Stir in the lemon juice, and all remaining ingredients. Mix well. Let sit for at least 1 hour before serving.

ONION-TOMATO RELISH

Makes approximately 12 fl oz/360 ml
26 Calories per tablespoon
0.1 g fat per tablespoon

A vibrant sweet and sour relish that is a perfect addition to barbecues and picnics.

4 oz/112 g raisins
4 fl oz/120 ml dark rum
20 large cloves garlic, peeled and
  sliced

6 fl oz/180 ml stock
1½ lb/675 g frozen pearl onions,
  unthawed
6 fl oz/180 ml apple juice
1 tin (1 lb/450 g) chopped Italian
  tomatoes
Salt and freshly ground pepper to
  taste

1 Combine the raisins and rum in a small bowl. Set aside.

2 Combine the garlic and 4 fl oz/120 ml stock in a large, heavy non-reactive frying pan. Boil, uncovered, until the stock is thick and syrupy and the garlic is very tender.

3 Add the frozen onions and 3 fl oz/90 ml apple juice. Simmer briskly, uncovered, until the mixture is almost dry and the onions are beginning to brown. Add the remaining apple juice and continue cooking, shaking the pan occasionally until the onions are browned and glazed.

4 Add a splash of stock. Simmer, shaking the frying pan for a few minutes until the onions are deeply and evenly browned.

5 Stir in the tomatoes, salt and pepper. Stir in the raisins and the rum. Simmer gently, covered, for 40 minutes, until the mixture is very thick and the onions are very tender. Uncover to stir occasionally. Add a bit of stock if the mixture gets thick too early and threatens to burn.

6 Store in the refrigerator. Serve at room temperature.

BRUSSELS SPROUTS IN DILL PESTO

Serves 6
60 Calories per serving
0.5 g fat

For a change, instead of serving good old sprouts, plainly steamed, try them cold, folded into a creamy, dill-flecked sauce. The sprouts and the yoghurt-herb paste may be prepared in advance. Add the fromage blanc and combine everything just before serving, or the dish will become watery.

---

1 large bag frozen button Brussels sprouts (do not thaw)	*3 tablespoons fromage blanc*
¾ pt/450 ml snipped dill leaves	*1 tablespoon raspberry vinegar, or wine vinegar*
½ pt/300 ml roughly chopped parsley	*Salt and freshly ground pepper to taste*
¼ lb/113 g yoghurt cheese (see page 27)	*Red lettuce or radicchio*
	Watercress

---

1   Steam the frozen sprouts over boiling water for 7–10 minutes, until cooked through but still a bit crunchy. Rinse under cold running water, drain well and chill.
2   Combine the dill, parsley and yoghurt cheese in the container of a food processor. Process to a thick paste. Stir in the fromage blanc and vinegar.
3   Combine the dill sauce and the sprouts. Season to taste.
4   Serve on red lettuce or radicchio. Garnish with watercress.

Top right: Tortilla chips (page 198).
A tempting array of open sandwiches, from pizza (page 198)
to smoked salmon with tzatziki and dill (page 57).

Snacks and Sandwiches

'So we'll just investigate the icebox as we have
done so oft at midnight . . . and all that it will be,
I do assure you, will be something swift and
quick and ready, something instant and felicitous,
and quite delicate and dainty – just a snack!'

Thomas Wolfe, *Of Time and the River*, 1935

*Mixed summer fruits are delicious topped with
fromage frais and caramelized brown sugar.*

It's the cravings and snackings and in-between munchings that get you into trouble. Little crispy fried things scoffed down in frightening quantity; butter- and mayonnaise-smeared sandwiches overstuffed with fatty meats; oily, sausage-festooned pizzas; 'fun' foods, but so bad for your weight maintenance and your health. Apply Slim Cuisine techniques to your snacking, and you can still have fun. After all, a sandwich is one of the friendliest edible objects in the world. There's something about two pieces of bread slapped together with interesting (and sometimes eccentric) ingredients that can cheer up the dourest snacker. Why deprive yourself? And why miss out on crispy little munchies, on pizza, on nachos? Read on.

Breads

Small pitta	*50 Calories each* *0.3 g fat*
Rye bread	*56 Calories per slice* *0.3 g fat*
Granary bread	*50 Calories per slice* *0.4 g fat*
Black bread	*79 Calories per slice* *0.4 g fat*
Wholemeal bread	*47 Calories per slice* *0.6 g fat*

Slim Sandwiches

For your sandwiches use a good wholegrain sliced bakery loaf that has some character, a crusty rye or a moist black bread.

Sliced chicken (roasted, poached or smoked)
Tomatoes
Pesto

Tzatziki
Smoked salmon

Sliced Cucumber
Dill pesto

Liptauer cheese
Sliced turkey

Lamb meatballs or kofta curry
Raita (cucumber or mint)
Served in pitta bread pockets

Italian sausage balls
Tomato sauce
Stir-'fried' or grilled peppers
Served in pitta bread pockets or rolls

Dill chicken salad
Sliced tomatoes

194

Tonnato
Roasted peppers

Russian dressing
Coleslaw
Sliced chicken

Hummus
Sliced tomatoes
Chopped parsley

Curried chicken salad
Chopped fresh coriander
Sliced mango

Peppered goose skirt steak slices
Browned onions or sweet and sour
    onions
Mustard

Pan-sautéed chicken cutlet
Stir-'fried' peppers

SLIM REUBEN

Sliced smoked chicken
Rinsed and drained sauerkraut
Thinly sliced Mozzarella

Slim Cuisine Russian dressing
    ('mayonnaise' mixed with a bit
    of tomato paste)

Toast this sandwich in a sandwich toaster

CLUB SANDWICH

Slim Cuisine 'mayonnaise'
Smoked chicken
Sliced tomato
Lettuce

Toast the bread first

SUMMER SANDWICH

Tomatoes
Quark or thinly-sliced Mozzarella
Fresh basil and chopped garlic

A light sprinkling of excellent wine
    vinegar (optional)

LUXURIOUS SUMMER SANDWICH

Chop together fresh basil, fresh garlic and Parmesan cheese, and
put this mixture on one slice of wholegrain bread. Top with sliced
ripe tomatoes and thin slices of Mozzarella. Spread the top piece of

bread with Crema di Pomodoro (sun-dried tomato paste: see page 45).

Toast this sandwich in a sandwich toaster.

PIZZA SANDWICH

Thinly sliced Mozzarella cheese
Tomato sauce
Crumbled dried oregano
Add if desired:
Crumbled dried chilli peppers

A spoonful of sautéed mushrooms
(see page 26)
A few slices of peeled red and yellow
peppers

Toast this sandwich in a sandwich toaster

VEGETARIAN SANDWICH 1

Beetroot Purée (see page 164) or
Beetroots in Mustard Sauce (see
page 163)

Watercress

VEGETARIAN SANDWICH 2

Chopped fresh spinach (raw)
Sliced mushrooms (raw)

Dijon mustard mixed with yoghurt

Use black bread for this sandwich

GOOD SPREADS FOR HONEST BREAD

These are marvellous on slices of toasted granary or rye bread.

Garlic spread (quark mixed with
baked garlic purée and a touch
of finely grated Parmesan. Vary
with grated nutmeg, chopped

fresh herbs, or chopped chives or
spring onions)

Beetroot Purée (see page 164)

Duxelles (see page 168)

ELLE GALE'S SARDINE FISH CREAM

Makes ⅖ pt
22.8 Calories per tablespoon
0.9 g fat

This is best with the goat's milk curd cheese from Beck Farm, Elle's place in Histon, near Cambridge but it's also good with quark, or any other low-fat curd cheese. Mash together 4 oz/112 g quark or other low-fat curd cheese with the contents of a 4-oz/112-g tin of sardines in tomato sauce (check the label and make sure it contains no oil). Stir in 2 teaspoons chopped chives; 2 spring onions, chopped; 3 drops reduced-salt Worcestershire sauce; 1 teaspoon lemon juice; salt and pepper to taste.

CHEESE ON TOAST

Lightly toast a piece of rye bread. Halve a clove of garlic. Rub the hot toast with the garlic. Cover the toast thinly with sliced Mozzarella cheese. Grill for 2–3 minutes until melted and speckled with brown. Sprinkle lightly with Hungarian paprika. Devour at once.

'Many the long night I've dreamed of cheese – toasted, mostly.'

Robert Louis Stevenson, *Treasure Island*, 1883

STRAWBERRY CREAM FOR BREAKFAST OR TEA

This is a splendid substitute for butter, Devonshire cream or whipped cream and strawberry jam. Spread it on scones, bread or toast for an unbelievably delicious low-Calorie snack. It tastes indulgent and luxurious, but contains just a fraction of the Calories of real cream and jam.

Very ripe (or overripe) strawberries
Skimmed-milk quark

Mash the strawberries with a fork. With a wooden spoon, beat the strawberries into the quark. Scrape into a bowl or crock, cover with cling film and refrigerate for a few hours for the flavours to blend. This will keep for several days and improve in flavour each day.

PIZZA

Pizza, with its gooey cheese and spicy sauce, may not be elegant, but it is one of the most satisfying dishes in the world. Happily, it is also one of the healthiest, if you avoid additions such as sausage, ham and other fatty meats.

When you are eating pizza out, (at one of the wonderful Pizza Express restaurants, for example,) specify that your pizza be prepared with no oil and no salt. The pizza will still be sumptuous, yet your Slim Cuisine regime will stay intact.

It's fun to make pizza at home and easy too if you begin with pitta bread as your base. Leave the pitta as it is or, to cut the calories even more, split each pitta into two rounds. Place the pitta on the grill tray (if they are split, place them smooth side down). Smear with Slim Cuisine Tomato Sauce (see page 151) and top with thin slices of part-skimmed Mozzarella cheese. Use the Italian brands that come packed in water. If you wish, top the tomato sauce with Sautéed Mushrooms, Browned Onions, Sliced Meatballs or Stir-'Fried' Peppers (see page 162) before laying on the cheese. Sprinkle on a little oregano. Have the grill set to its highest heat and place the grill tray in the lowest position. Grill for 3–4 minutes until the cheese is nicely gooey and runny. Eat with pleasure and no guilt at all.

Mushroom Pizza with whole pitta:	130 Calories
	4.9 g fat
Mushroom Pizza with split pitta:	105 Calories
	4.7 g fat

CORN TORTILLAS AND TORTILLA CHIPS

63 Calories per *whole* tortilla
0.6 g fat

Tortilla chips, sometimes called nacho chips (totopos in Mexico) are very popular as snack food. They are compelling munchies on their own, or as paddles for dips. Alas, they are always fried and often oversalted too. If you can find tortillas in your supermarket or local deli, you can make your own healthy tortilla chips; no frying and only as much salt as you want. Look for wide, flat, yellow and red cans of Old El Paso corn tortillas. Bake as many tortillas as you like, in one layer, on the shelf of your oven at 400° F (200° C/Gas Mark 6) for 3–4 minutes until crisp. Remove and break into eighths. (Alternatively, for neater pieces, cut the tortillas in quarters or eighths with scissors *before* baking. Spread the pieces directly on the oven shelf.) Sprinkle with a bit of salt, or chilli powder, paprika, cumin, whatever you like. Or leave unseasoned, so that the pure and heady maize taste comes through. Store in an airtight biscuit tin. Eat as they are, use with dips, or consider one of the following:

TOSTADAS

222 Calories
5.9 g fat

1   Spread *whole* baked tortillas with Chilli con Carne (see page 101) and sprinkle with shredded Mozzarella. Grill for 1–2 minutes, to melt the cheese. Serve at once.
2   Spread the whole baked tortilla with mashed, cooked beans (black beans or kidney beans) that have been seasoned with salt, ground cumin and chilli powder. Sprinkle with shredded Mozzarella. Grill as above. Serve at once. (153 Calories, 5.2 g fat.)
3   Spread with mashed beans (see 2, above) that have been thinned with a bit of stock and gently warmed. Top with crisp, shredded lettuce, a dollop of fromage blanc, and finely chopped red and yellow peppers. (89 Calories, 0.7 g fat.)

NACHOS AL CARBON

75 Calories
3.3 g fat

Break the baked tortillas into quarters (or cut them into quarters with scissors before you bake them). Spread in one layer on a baking tray or ovenproof platter. Put a dollop of mashed beans (see above) on each. Top each with a slice of Peppered Goose Skirt Steak, with or without the Mushroom Sauce (see page 107). Top with shredded Mozzarella. Grill for 1 minute to melt the cheese. Add a dab of fromage blanc and some Salsa if you wish (see page 170). Place the tray in the middle of the table and let everyone grab and munch.

Desserts

'Now you can eat all the pudding you want and not end up like one.'

David Gelef, *Punch*, October 1985

You've heard it a thousand times: puddings and sweets are evil, they will rot your teeth, pad your hips and probably initiate moral disintegration. Don't believe it! I have a wonderful surprise for you: a whole clutch of indulgent and flossy desserts that will contribute not an iota to the decay of your teeth, your litheness or your good character. These sweets are all visual knockouts, as well as delicious. Some are 'nouvelle' in character, others endearingly old-fashioned, but each will end a meal with a flourish.

Dessert Guidelines

1   Desserts should always be considered a significant and important component of a meal, not a cholesterol-, fat- and Calorie-laden 'reward' for finishing all your vegetables. Plan your desserts so that they contribute valuable nutrients along with their Calories. Worthless Calories are a Slim Cuisine no-no.

2   A little bit of sugar every once in a while will not hurt. Just remember that sugar should always be a light seasoning to be used by the sprinkle; not a major ingredient to be used by the handful. Nutrasweet (Canderel) is extremely low in Calories and has no aftertaste. It can be used in recipes that do not call for high heat. (When heated, the sweetness in Nutrasweet dissipates.) Whichever you choose, use it in moderation. It is a good idea to alternate sweeteners, so that you do not overload on one or the other. If you decide to substitute sugar for Nutrasweet in any of these recipes, you will be adding 34 Calories per tablespoonful of sugar to the Calorie count of the finished dish.

3   High-quality unsweetened frozen fruits and berries are available in exhilarating profusion in supermarkets, and in freezer stores (like Bejam). Keep your freezer stocked at all times with a good variety. Many splendid, nutritious desserts can be made in minutes with a generous supply at hand. Also keep on hand a selection of low-fat dairy products: yoghurt, fromage blanc, buttermilk, skimmed milk, etc.

'Cecily (sweetly):   Sugar?
Gwendolyn (superciliously):   No, thank you. Sugar is not
                        fashionable any more.'

Oscar Wilde, *The Importance of Being Earnest*, 1895

Icecreams and Sorbets

Slim Cuisine icecreams are so creamy, so vividly fruity and out-rageously voluptuous that you will feel delightful pangs of guilt as you polish off a large serving. Not to worry. They are nutrient-dense and Calorie-shy. It's okay to indulge. Make them, serve them and eat them. They do not store well. (These recipes can be halved, if desired.) Use these ideas as guidelines and invent your own versions.

BANANA ICECREAM

Serves 6
93 Calories per serving
0.2 g fat

Cut peeled bananas into 1-in/2.5-cm chunks, and cut each chunk in half. Spread on a baking tray and freeze. When frozen, remove to a plastic bag and store in the freezer until you want to make icecream.

4 frozen bananas, cut into chunks	3–4 tablespoons Nutrasweet
½ teaspoon vanilla essence	(Canderel)
	5 fl oz/150 ml buttermilk

1　Place the frozen banana chunks in the container of the food processor. Add the vanilla, sweetener and half the buttermilk.
2　Turn on the processor and let it run for a few moments. Then, while it is running, pour in the remaining buttermilk in a thin, steady stream. Let the machine run until the mixture is beauti-fully smooth and creamy. Spoon into bowls and serve at once.

BANANA GINGER ICECREAM

As for Banana Icecream, but omit vanilla essence. Add a scant teaspoon of grated fresh ginger and, if you wish, a splash of dark rum.

RASPBERRY ICECREAM

43 Calories per serving
0.3 g fat

My colleague, Ginny Broad, serves this to guests mounded in

melon halves. It's an impressive and colourful finish to a dinner party.

1 12-oz/335-g packet frozen raspberries (unsweetened)	*6–8 fl oz/240 ml cold buttermilk* *4–5 tablespoons Nutrasweet (Canderel)*

1   Do not thaw the berries. Dump them, still frozen, into the bowl of a food processor or liquidizer. Pour in half of the buttermilk and sprinkle in the sweetener.
2   Turn on the machine. Process for a few seconds, stopping to scrape down the sides if necessary.
3   With the machine running, pour in the remaining buttermilk. Process until the mixture forms a super-creamy icecream. Spoon into clear glass goblets and serve *at once*.

Variations:
1   Strawberry Icecream (32 Calories, 0.3 g fat per serving). Substitute frozen strawberries for the raspberries.
2   Strawberry-Orange Icecream (40 Calories, 0.3 g fat per serving). Add the pulp, juice and grated zest of an orange to the berries in Step 1.
3   Apple Icecream (39 Calories, 0.2 g fat per serving). Substitute frozen apple pieces and a frozen banana cut into chunks for the raspberries. Add a sprinkling of cinnamon.

PINEAPPLE SORBET

46 Calories per serving
0.1 g of fat

For this wonderfully refreshing recipe you need frozen pineapple cubes. Buy ripe pineapples, peel and cube them, discarding the tough core, and freeze the cubes flat on baking trays. When thoroughly frozen, transfer to plastic bags. When you want to make sorbet, remove the amount you need. If the cubes have frozen together in the bag, so that you have a solid mass, drop the bag on the floor a few times to separate them.

Frozen pineapple cubes	*A splash or two of dark rum*

1   Place the frozen pineapple cubes and the rum in the container of the food processor. Turn the machine on. It will rattle and clatter and leap all over the counter. Steady it and allow it to

run, stopping occasionally to scrape down the sides with a rubber spatula, until it is of a sorbet consistency. Serve at once.

'Tastes and odours can never be described unless they are comparable with known tastes and odours and the mango is unique and completely superior. It may be peeled and eaten out of hand, gnawing at last on the great pit; it may be cut daintily and served just so.'

Marjorie Kinnan Rawlings, *Cross Creek*, 1942

MANGO SORBET

Approx. 66 Calories per ½ mango serving
0.4 g fat

You haven't lived until you've tasted Mango Sorbet. Use it as a stunning finish to an elegant dinner, or serve it for a private indulgence. The mango cubes can be frozen months ahead of time. (Make sure that you use really ripe mangoes.) The sorbet itself must be prepared just before serving. It's very easy and very quick. Simply excuse yourself, retire to the food processor, whip it up, and serve it forth proudly. Your guests will admire your talent and ingenuity.

Frozen mango cubes (see below) *A sprinkle of Nutrasweet and a*
A splash or 2 of dark rum (optional) *tablespoon of buttermilk, if*
necessary

---

1   With a sharp knife slice down on each whole mango as if you were slicing it in half, but try to miss the large flat centre stone. Slice down again on the other side of the stone. You will now have 2 half mangoes and the flat centre stone to which quite a bit of mango flesh clings.
2   With a small, sharp paring knife score each mango half lengthwise and crosswise, cutting all the way to, but not through the skin. Push out the skin as if you were pushing the half mango inside out. The mango flesh will stand out in cubes. Slice these cubes off the skin.
3   With the knife, remove the skin from the mango flesh remaining on the stone. Slice the flesh off the stone. Spread all the mango cubes and pieces on a flat tray and freeze. When frozen solid, transfer to plastic bags. Pull out the bags when you are ready to make the sorbet. If the cubes have frozen together in the bag, so that you have a solid mass, drop it on the floor a few times.

4   To make the sorbet, place the frozen mango cubes and the optional rum in the container of a food processor. Turn the machine on. It will rattle and clatter all over the counter. Steady it and allow it to run, stopping occasionally to scrape down the sides with a rubber spatula. It will seem quite splintery at first. Taste for sweetness. If necessary, add a sprinkling of Nutrasweet, but if the mangoes were really ripe it probably won't be necessary. Continue processing and if the mango does not seem to be coming to sorbet consistency add 1–2 tablespoons (no more) of buttermilk. When the mixture reaches a very smooth sorbet consistency, place several small balls of the sorbet on each plate. Garnish with mint leaves. (In the summer, a scattering of raspberries, blackberries and other berries can be arranged on the plate as well.)

Variation:

This recipe works very well with ripe cantaloupe too, Remove the melon flesh with a teaspoon or a melon baller and freeze the pieces flat, then transfer to plastic bags.

'One of those musty fragrant, deep-ribbed cantaloups, chilled to the heart now, in all their pink-flesh taste and ripeness . . . or a bowl of those red raspberries, most luscious and most rich'

Thomas Wolfe, *Time and the River*, 1935

BLUEBERRY ICECREAM

Serves 6
41 Calories per serving
0.3 g fat

For this brilliantly coloured icecream, squirrel away blueberries in the freezer. In season, buy them in profusion, freeze them flat on trays, then transfer to plastic bags. Blueberries are usually sweet enough – but you may need the barest sprinkle of sweetener.

---

12 oz/335 g frozen blueberries	Nutrasweet (Canderel) (optional)
6–8 fl oz/240 ml cold buttermilk	

---

1   Do not thaw the berries. Dump them, still frozen, into the bowl of a processor or liquidizer. Pour in half of the buttermilk.
2   Turn on the machine. Process for a few seconds, stopping to scrape down the sides if necessary. Taste. Add a bit of Canderel if needed. Pour in the remaining buttermilk. Process

206

until the mixture forms a super-creamy icecream. Spoon into clear glass goblets and serve *at once*.

More Icecream Ideas:

Frozen peaches flavoured with almond or vanilla essence, or try combinations: pineapple/orange; raspberry/melon; banana/strawberry.

SLIM 'WHIPPED CREAM'

300 Calories per entire recipe
0.4 g fat

In summer months seasonal fruits or berries with a creamy topping make an elegant, hard-to-improve finale to a meal. Here is the simplest (and one of the best). Quickly and gently rinse some strawberries in a colander under running water. Shake dry. Put them, in a bowl, on the table. Give everyone a small bowl of fromage blanc and an even smaller bowl of dark brown sugar (1 tablespoon or less). Let everyone pick up a berry by its green top, dip it into the fromage blanc, then into sugar. Eating these delectable morsels is pure summer pleasure. If you want to get a bit more elegant, try the following topping for fresh berries or sliced peaches, or whatever you like – it's *better* than whipped cream.

---

8 fl oz/240 ml fromage blanc
¼ teaspoon vanilla essence
2 egg whites, at room temperature

Pinch of salt
2 tablespoons sugar

---

1   Mix together the fromage blanc and vanilla.
2   In a spotlessly clean bowl, with a wire whip, beat the egg whites with the salt until they are foamy. Add sugar, a little at a time, and continue beating until the egg whites are shiny and hold firm peaks.
3   Fold the beaten egg whites into the fromage blanc.

BLACKBERRY GRATIN

Serves 8
82 Calories per serving
0.8 g fat

This old-fashioned, juicy-purple fruit pudding is one of my all-time favourites. Because it uses frozen berries, it can be enjoyed all the year round. A summertime recipe for fruit gratin, using fresh berries, follows. I like to serve this lukewarm, but it's good at room temperature as well, and it's good cold. And leftovers served right from the fridge make a splendid breakfast.

1 lb/450 g frozen blackberries, thawed	1 tablespoon ground toasted skinned hazelnuts
2 rounded tablespoons brown sugar	½ pt/300 ml low-fat fromage blanc
2 tablespoons dry coarse wholewheat breadcrumbs	

1   Preheat the grill to its highest point.
2   Thoroughly mix the thawed berries with one tablespoon of brown sugar, the crumbs and the ground nuts. Spread the mixture into a non-reactive, oval or round 1-pt/600-ml gratin dish.
3   Spread the fromage blanc smoothly and evenly over the berries. Sprinkle the top with the remaining tablespoon of brown sugar.
4   Grill not too close to the heating element or flame for 4–5 minutes, until the mixture is bubbly and the sugar caramelized. Allow to cool slightly. Spoon into glass bowls and serve.

FRESH BERRY GRATIN

Approx. 72 Calories per serving
0.3 g fat

Use whole raspberries, whole blueberries, halved strawberries, etc. The berries and part of the fromage blanc remain cool, but the topping becomes hot and bubbly. It is a most pleasing contrast.

Berries	Brown sugar
Fromage blanc	

1   Preheat grill.
2   Spread the berries in a gratin dish.
3   Spread fromage blanc evenly over the berries. Sprinkle evenly with 1–2 tablespoons dark brown sugar.
4   Grill close to the heating element for 1 minute, until the sugar is melted and bubbly. Serve *at once*.

STRAWBERRIES ON RED AND WHITE SAUCE

52 Calories for entire recipe
0.4 g fat

This very beautiful dessert would make a perfect ending to a special dinner party. The presentation is inspired by *nouvelle cuisine*, the Calories are minimal.

Fresh, ripe strawberries	*Buttermilk*
Raspberry sauce (see recipe)	*Mint leaves*

---

1 Hull the strawberries.
2 Use clear glass plates if possible. Pour some raspberry sauce on one half of the plate. Pour some buttermilk on the other half.
3 Place strawberries in a row down the dividing line. Garnish with fresh mint leaves.

RASPBERRY SAUCE

Makes 16 fl oz/480 ml
12 Calories per tablespoon
0.1 g fat

This is a basic dessert sauce, useful in myriad ways. It can top icecreams, or be swirled into fromage blanc or yoghurt to create a fruit fool, or served as a dipping sauce for fresh whole strawberries.

---

2 boxes (12 oz/335 g each) frozen	*Nutrasweet (Canderel) to taste*
raspberries, thawed and drained	

---

1 Purée the berries in the liquidizer.
2 Pour into a sieve and rub through. Discard the seeds.
3 Stir in sweetener (2–3 tablespoons) to taste. Refrigerate until needed.

Variations:

Substitute other fruit – frozen blackcurrants, strawberries or blackberries – for the raspberries. Sweeten to taste. The Blackcurrant Sauce is wonderful enough to serve as a pudding all by itself (or perhaps topped with a dollop of low-fat fromage blanc).

MANGO SAUCE

Place cubed, fresh, ripe mango (see Mango Sorbet, page 205 for procedure) into the jar of the liquidizer. Purée until perfectly smooth. To end a summer meal on a sublime note, pour a puddle of Mango Sauce on each dessert plate. Heap a generous serving of raspberries on each puddle. Top with a cloud of Slim Cuisine 'Whipped Cream' (see page 207). When raspberries are out of season, substitute peeled, sliced kiwi fruit.

CRUNCHY BANANAS ON RED AND WHITE SAUCE

Serves 4
96 Calories per serving
0.9 g fat

Kids love this, and adults won't complain either. The buttermilk, combined with the sauce, tastes deceptively rich and creamy.

1 rounded tablespoon low-fat fromage blanc or yoghurt	1 heaped tablespoon dry wholewheat breadcrumbs
½ tablespoon ground, toasted, skinned hazelnuts	2 bananas
	Buttermilk
	Strawberry Sauce (see page 209)

1   Preheat the grill to its highest point. Line the grill pan with foil, shiny side up. Place a rack on the pan.
2   Put the fromage blanc on a plate. Mix the nuts and crumbs on another plate.
3   Cut each banana in half lengthwise. Cut each half into 5 pieces.
4   Dip the top side of each banana piece in the fromage blanc. Then dredge it in the crumbs. Place on the grill rack crumbed side up.
5   Grill on the lowest shelf for 3–4 minutes, until crispy on top.
6   Pour some strawberry sauce on half the surface of a small plate. Pour some buttermilk on the other half. Place 5 banana pieces down the centre. Serve at once.

GINGER LIME MOUSSE

Serves 6
82 Calories per serving
0.2 g fat

This mousse is exquisitely subtle and fragrant. Serve it to your gastronome friends as a finale to a very special dinner party. It's the sort of thing that should be eaten slowly and lingeringly so that every nuance can be savoured.

---

4 fl oz/120 ml water
2 rounded tablespoons grated fresh
  ginger root
Grated zest of 1 lime
Juice of 1 lime

1 sachet gelatine
6 tablespoons Nutrasweet
  (Canderel)
16 fl oz/480 ml low-fat fromage
  blanc
8 fl oz/240 ml buttermilk

---

1 Combine the water, ginger and lime zest in a saucepan. Simmer for 5 minutes. Stir in the lime juice. Remove from the heat. Stir in the gelatine.
2 Cool to room temperature.
3 When cooled, strain the mixture, pressing down on the solids to extract their flavour. Stir the sweetener into the strained mixture until it is dissolved.
4 Place the fromage blanc and the sweetened mixture into the container of the food processor, or liquidizer. Process until perfectly smooth. While the machine is running, pour in the buttermilk in a steady stream.
5 Pour and scrape the mixture into an attractive serving dish or into 6 individual glass goblets. Chill for several hours or overnight.

ALMOND CURD WITH BLACKCURRANT SAUCE

Serves 6
88 Calories per serving
0.2 g fat

I borrowed the Almond Curd from Chinese Cuisine, and added a dollop of fragrant Blackcurrant Sauce. The combination is stunning and deeply soothing.

1 sachet gelatine
12 fl oz/360 ml hot water
12 fl oz/360 ml skimmed milk
½ teaspoon pure almond essence

¼ teaspoon pure vanilla essence
6 tablespoons Canderel
  (Nutrasweet)
Blackcurrant Sauce (see page 209)

1   Mix the gelatine into the hot water. Stir until thoroughly
    dissolved. Stir in milk, and almond and vanilla essences. Cool
    to room temperature.
2   When cooled, add the sweetener. Stir until it is dissolved.
3   Pour the mixture into a shallow 2-pt/1,200-ml baking pan and
    chill for several hours, or overnight, until set.
4   To serve, spoon into shallow goblets. Top with a dollop of
    Blackcurrant Sauce.

TROPICAL FRUIT JELLY

Serves 6
110 Calories per serving
0.45 g fat

A refreshing jelly, evocative of sunshine both in taste and colour. It
is a very soft jelly, not at all rubbery, so serve it in bowls, rather
than trying to mould it. Passion fruit is ripe when it is wrinkled and
wizened looking; mango when it is soft to the touch and fragrant. It
is impossible to say how much sweetener will be needed; it
depends on the fruit and juices, so taste as you go.

24 fl oz/720 ml fresh orange juice
2 fl oz/60 ml lime juice
2 tablespoons plain gelatine
Approx. 4 tablespoons Canderel
  (Nutrasweet)

4 passion fruit
2 ripe mangoes

1   In a saucepan combine 4 fl oz/120 ml of orange juice with the
    lime juice. Sprinkle the gelatine over the juices. Stir over low
    heat until warm and dissolved. Do not let it come to a simmer.
2   Pour the remaining orange juice into a bowl. Stir in the
    gelatine mixture. Taste and add a tablespoon or so of sweet-
    ener if the juice is particularly acid. If the orange juice is sweet,
    you may need no sweetener at all, or only a sprinkle. Chill the
    mixture for an hour or so, until thickened but not set.
3   Meanwhile cut the passion fruit in half, and scoop the pulp,
    seeds and all, into the liquidizer container. Cut the mangoes in
    half (over a bowl, to catch the juices) and scoop out the flesh

(see page 205 for procedure). Add mango flesh and juices to the liquidizer. Purée briefly. Push through a non-reactive sieve to eliminate the passion fruit seeds.

4   Thoroughly stir the puréed mixture into the thickened juice. Taste and add sweetener to taste. Stir thoroughly to dissolve.
5   Return to the refrigerator for another hour or so, until set. Serve spooned into glass goblets.

Variation:
Omit the passion fruit and use only mangoes, if desired. Instead of puréeing them, process them until they are finely chopped. Stir into the jelly in Step 4.

APRICOT JAM

Makes 1⅕ pts/720 ml
24 Calories per tablespoon
0 g fat

1 lb/450 g dried apricots	*2 tablespoons brandy*

1   Put the apricots in a heavy saucepan. Add water to generously cover. Bring to simmer.
2   Cook over low heat, stirring frequently, until the apricots lose their shape and cook into a lumpy mass. This will take anything from 15 minutes to 1 hour, depending on the fruit.
3   Stir in the brandy and a few more ounces of water. Cook for a few more minutes, stirring, until the mixture is very thick. Be careful not to scorch the mixture. Cool.
4   Taste. If the mixture is too tart, stir in a bit of Canderel or sugar. If too sweet, stir in a few drops of fresh lemon juice. Scrape the mixture into a crock or bowl. Cover tightly and refrigerate. It will keep for weeks.

APRICOT CREAM

Fold together equal parts of Apricot Jam and low-fat fromage blanc. If desired, sprinkle each portion with a few toasted pine kernels.

Menu Planning

'For supper Jill cooks a filet of sole, lemony, light, simmered in sunshine, skin flaky brown. Nelson gets a hamburger with wheatgerm sprinkled on it to remind him of a Nutburger. Wheatgerm, zucchini, water chestnuts, celery salt, Familia: these are some of the exotic items Jill's shopping brings into the house.'

John Updike, *Rabbit Redux*, 1973

Changing over to Slim Cuisine means learning some new techniques and habits. It takes no longer to do Slim Cuisine than any other kind of everyday cookery, especially if you plan ahead. Always keep a supply of baked aubergine and baked garlic purée in the fridge, for instance. Then, if you want to make meatballs or pesto, you don't have to begin first baking the aubergine and the garlic before getting down to the business of the recipe itself. And Slim Cuisine icecream is the fastest pudding imaginable if the freezer is well stocked with frozen fruit and berries. You must keep these things on board as well: stock or a good stock powder, and drained yoghurt and/or drained fromage blanc. Plan ahead, keep these things on hand, and cooking will be a breeze.

Calorie Note:
All menus fall in the 400–600 Calorie range per person for the entire meal.

Dinner Parties

All too often, dinner parties are excuses for total culinary depravity. Creamed sauces, roasts with thick layers of fat, rich gravies, vegetables swimming in butter, sugary puddings drowning in oceans of double cream: it is almost as if the hostess/cook says: 'The Robinsons are coming to dinner. Let's *kill* them!' As a devotee of Slim Cuisine, you know that culinary mayhem is obsolete, even at dinner parties. It is possible to entertain lavishly and deliciously without Calorie and fat overkill. Herewith a few suggestions:

Turkey and melon with mint pesto   (page 57)
Wild mushroom soup   (page 72)
Stuffed rolled skirt steak   (page 109)
Potato gratin   (page 173)
Stir-'fried' courgettes   (page 159)
Mango sorbet   (page 205)

Mushroom ravioli with green sauce   (page 53)
Jellied gazpacho   (page 76)
Grilled plaice with mustard   (page 82)
Braised fennel   (page 165)
Steamed broccoli   (page 165)
Blackberry gratin   (page 207)

Steamed asparagus on yellow pepper sauce   (page 161)
Herbed tomato soup   (page 63)
Pork medallions esterhazy   (page 110)
Roast potatoes   (page 176)
Strawberries on red and white sauce   (page 209)

Poached mushrooms stuffed with mint raita
and beet purée   (page 52)
Soup of baked vegetables   (page 70)
Steak with garlic wine sauce   (page 104)
Stir-'fried' cauliflower   (page 160)
Stuffed potatoes   (page 171)
Blueberry icecream   (page 206)

Tuna mousse   (page 56)
Onion soup   (page 69)
Chicken with yellow pepper sauce   (page 119)
Creamed spinach   (page 163)
Potato cases filled with mushroom ragout   (page 172)
Tropical fruit jelly   (page 212)

215

Vegetarian Dinner Parties

Ethnic Feasts

For a wonderful dinner party, try a buffet of ethnic delicacies. The ethnic recipes in Slim Cuisine are all based on authentic ones, but they have been redesigned to eliminate fat. Even though the identifying fat of a particular cuisine is gone (lard for Mexico, olive oil for Italy, etc.) the remaining flavour principles are unchanged.

Mexican

Salsa with tortilla chips	(page 170)
Frijol-albondiga casserole	(page 91)
Chilaquiles	(page 129)
Stir-'fried' courgettes with lime and cumin	(page 159)
Mango sorbet	(page 205)

Italian

Tomato-Mozzarella salad	(page 185)
Italian sausage balls served with tomato	(page 94)
sauce and a dollop of pesto surrounded by:	(page 145)
Stir-'fried' peppers and browned onions	(page 162)
Sweet and sour courgettes	(page 160)
Braised fennel	(page 165)
Fresh berry gratin	(page 208)

Vegetarian Italian

Tomato-Mozzarella salad	(page 185)
Pasta quills tossed in pesto	(page 145)
Braised cauliflower	(page 157)
Braised fennel	(page 165)
Mushroom ragout	(page 167)
Fresh berry gratin	(page 208)

French

Onion soup	(page 69)
Chicken braised with garlic	(page 124)
Mashed potato gratin	(page 173)
Poached mushroom caps stuffed with duxelles	(page 52)
Fresh berry gratin	(page 208)

Indian

Aloo chat	(page 60)
Kofta curry	(page 92)
Chicken curry	(page 121)
Raita	(page 183)
Vegetable bhaji	(page 156)
Spicy lentils	(page 179)
Ginger lime mousse	(page 211)

Vegetarian Indian

Aloo chat	(page 60)
Vegetable bhaji	(page 156)
Spicy lentils	(page 179)
Curried roast potatoes	(page 176)
Raita	(page 183)
Ginger lime mousse	(page 211)

Everyday and Family Meals

Everyday cooking needn't be elaborate; in fact, it shouldn't be. A hearty main dish and perhaps a salad or a vegetable and a good pudding should be more than enough. I'm particularly fond of family-type dishes that fill the house with heavenly aromas as they bubble happily away, in the oven or on the hob.

Italian sausage soup	(page 74)
Tomato-basil salad	(page 185)
Strawberry icecream	(page 204)
Shepherd's pie	(page 97)
Creamed spinach or	(page 163)
Cole slaw	(page 188)
Crunchy bananas	(page 210)
Carrot soup	(page 68)
Baked potatoes with a choice of fillings	(page 169)
Raspberry icecream	(page 203)
Hamburgers with browned onions and red pepper sauce	(page 96)
Cole slaw	(page 188)
Apple icecream	(page 204)
Oven-'fried' fish	(page 83)
Oven chips	(page 175)
Selected greens with creamy salad dressing	(page 182)
Banana icecream	(page 203)

Vegetarian Family Meals

Larder lasagne	(page 135)
Tomato salad with creamy dressing	(page 182)
Blueberry icecream	(page 206)
Rajmaa (bean casserole)	(page 137)

Tabouli (page 189)
Blackberry gratin (page 207)

Quick Meals

For those who work full time, and then come home to cook, weekday meals *must* be quick. There are a wealth of quick, delicious and deeply satisfying dishes to choose from. It seems a shame to have to succumb to the lure of packaged and frozen foods because of limited time. Try the following suggestions or make your own prepared meals by freezing small portions of chilli con carne, beef in red wine, shepherd's pie, bolognese sauce, lasagne, etc. to be microwaved when needed.

Steak and onions (page 109)
Steamed broccoli (page 165)
Strawberry-orange icecream (page 204)

Pizza (page 198)
Sweet and sour courgettes (page 160)
Pineapple sorbet (page 204)

Plaice en papillote (page 84)
Steamed new potatoes
Fresh berry gratin (page 208)

Spaghetti bolognese (page 102)
Wholemeal toast and garlic spread (page 196)
Strawberries with raspberry sauce (page 209)

Vegetarian Quick Meals

Pasta with terracotta sauce (page 147)
Steamed cauliflower
Apple icecream (page 204)

Farmer's omelette (page 136)
Beets (use cooked beets from the market)
in mustard cream (page 163)
Sliced bananas or peaches with a
sprinkle of brown sugar

Pasta shells Alfredo (page 141)
Poached mushroom caps (unfilled) (page 52)
Raspberry icecream (page 203)

Index

223